THE
RODCHENKOV
AFFAIR

THE
RODCHENKOV
AFFAIR

How I Brought Down Putin's
Secret Doping Empire

DR GRIGORY
RODCHENKOV

ALLEN

1 3 5 7 9 10 8 6 4 2

WH Allen, an imprint of Ebury Publishing,
20 Vauxhall Bridge Road,
London SW1V 2SA

WH Allen is part of the Penguin Random House group of companies whose
addresses can be found at global.penguinrandomhouse.com

Penguin
Random House
UK

First published in the United Kingdom by WH Allen in 2020

www.penguin.co.uk

A CIP catalogue record for this book is available from the British Library

Hardback ISBN 9780753553329
Trade Paperback ISBN 9780753553336

Typeset in 12/18 pt Fleischman BT Pro by Jouve UK, Milton Keynes
Printed and bound in Great Britain by Clays Ltd, Elcograf S.p.A.

Penguin Random House is committed to a sustainable future for our business,
our readers and our planet. This book is made from Forest Stewardship
Council® certified paper.

CONTENTS

PART III: CONJURER 139

PART IV: EXILE 231

NOTE TO THE READER

By my definition, a 'whistle-blower' is a man who dwells in an ambiguous netherworld, where a perverse pride in his past unethical achievements coexists with a desire to expose the corrupt system that successfully nurtured him for so long.

What follows is not an attempt to make excuses for my actions, nor to justify them. It strives to be one thing above all: honest. I will not shy away from giving a full and candid account of what I did, and nor do I ask you to forgive me. For as George Orwell wrote, 'There was truth and there was untruth, and if you clung to the truth even against the whole world, you were not mad.'

Let's begin.

INTRODUCTION

I am in involuntary exile from my homeland, Russia. I live in protective custody in the proverbial 'undisclosed location', and whenever I leave my small apartment I am accompanied by one, or sometimes two, armed guards. On occasion, I wear a bullet-proof vest.

For much of my youth, I was a competitive runner; now when I want to jog or even go for a walk, I have to wait for someone to take me out, just as my dog used to when I lived in Moscow.

I fled Russia in November 2015, fearing for my life.

As an academic chemist trained in instrumental analysis, analytical chemistry and chemical kinetics, I helped run the most successful sport doping enterprise in world history. As director of Russia's ironically named Moscow Anti-Doping Centre, my job was to make sure that the hundreds of Russian athletes participating in international events were never caught with banned substances, such as anabolic steroids or synthetic testosterone, in their body fluids during training camps and competitions.

When we were at the height of our powers, there seemed to be nothing we could not do. 'Dirty' urine samples soaked with performance-enhancing drugs emerged 'clean' from my laboratory. For over ten years, and five Olympics, not one athlete under my guidance tested positive for doping substances during the competitions.

George Orwell wrote about 'doublethink', which he said was 'To know and not to know, to be conscious of complete truthfulness while telling carefully constructed lies.' I embody this Orwellian doublethink: I was dedicated to Soviet and Russian sport, yet I am denounced as a traitor in my own country. I am one of the reasons my country won so many Olympic medals from 2004–2014, yet I was also the cause of their banishment from the Olympic Movement.

I consider myself to be honest, yet I knowingly defrauded the world's anti-doping authorities for more than a decade, both for the greater 'glory' of Russian athletes and also to satisfy sports bureaucrats who were bent on perpetuating Russia's sporting success. I justified my actions to myself by explaining that there had never been any real doping control in the Soviet Union or in Russia, so I was simply continuing along a well-trodden path. At the same time, I had contempt for the international anti-doping authorities, who spouted high-minded rhetoric about 'clean sport' but – Orwell again – failed repeatedly to see what was in front of their nose. To my mind, they were never serious about cracking down on sport doping. Fans paid lots of money to watch elite athletes, both live and on TV, and sport didn't look broken. Why should they, or I, bother to fix it?

I am a devoted husband and father, but I haven't seen my wife and children in four years.

My name appears in international newspapers, but I am a ghost.

You have heard about the fox and the henhouse. Well, I was the fox. I built the henhouse. And then I ate the hens.

But I certainly didn't work alone – in fact, I administered Russia's doping operation under the close scrutiny of the secret police: the FSB, the former KGB. The Ministry of Sport monitored my every move. And all this took place under the watchful eye of the sport-obsessed judo fan himself, President Vladimir Putin.

Seven months prior to the 2014 Winter Olympic Games in Sochi, reports emerged of systematic cheating by Russian athletes. The details were initially murky, and the early whistle-blowers were former dopers who had dropped out of Russian sport. It would be two years before the full scope of Russia's state-sponsored, systematic doping programme came to light – a programme that had been part of the fabric of Soviet and Russian sport for decades.

Following the revelations after the Sochi Games, it became very inconvenient to be me. The World Anti-Doping Agency (WADA) and the International Olympic Committee (IOC) initiated full-blown investigations of the Russian sport hierarchy. My name appeared 97 times in a 2015 Independent Commission's Report, more than anyone else's – according to them, I was 'the heart of the positive drug test cover-up'. I was also famously identified as 'an aider and abettor of the doping activities'.

The massive doping scandal that would result in Russia's limited participation in the Rio de Janeiro Olympic Games in 2016, and their painful suspension from the Paralympic Games in 2016 and the Winter Games in Pyeongchang in 2018, exploded

into the world's headlines. This wasn't just a sporting contro-
versy; it was a geopolitical event. An irate President Putin
demanded 'personalised and absolute' accountability from the
perpetrators of the doping scheme. My face was in the centre of
the bull's eye – I had been director of the Moscow Anti-Doping
Centre since 2005, and I was in charge of the famously corrupt
Olympic laboratory at the Sochi Winter Games in 2014.

After I was forced to resign from the Anti-Doping Centre,
friends warned me that my life might be in danger. Facing possible expulsion from the Olympic Movement, the Putin regime
was eager to identify scapegoats and pretend it was fighting
against doping. When the Los Angeles-based filmmaker Bryan
Fogel, with whom I had been collaborating on the movie that
would become the Academy-Award-winning documentary
Icarus, offered me a ticket to the United States, I grabbed my
laptop and hard drive from my office, packed a carry-on bag
and fled.

It was a radical decision. I abandoned Veronika, my wife of 34
years, and my two adult children, Vasily and Marina. The *Sled-
kom*, as the Investigative Committee of the Russian Federation is
known, ransacked my apartment and interrogated my family.
They were safe; they knew nothing about any doping schemes
and had no idea where I kept my files.

But I feared for my life, fears that seemed justified when two
of my former colleagues, Vyacheslav Sinev, the former director of
the Russian Anti-Doping Agency (RUSADA), and his successor Dr Nikita Kamaev mysteriously died within 11 days of each
other. They knew plenty about athletes falsifying their doping

control samples by substituting thawed urine from the freezers. Nikita, a friend of mine from childhood, was a healthy sports enthusiast who exercised regularly. He supposedly succumbed to a heart attack at the age of 52, and was quickly buried with a pro forma autopsy. No one from the Ministry of Sport or the Russian Olympic Committee attended either man's funeral.

During my five years in exile, there have been credible threats on my life. Putin has declared that I'm an American intelligence agent and that I belong in jail. An arrest warrant was issued for me, and one of his allies, the former Russian Olympic Committee chief Leonid Tyagachev, stated that 'Rodchenkov should be shot for lying, like Stalin would have done.' My lawyers have been told that I rank among the top five on the Kremlin's worldwide hit list.

As I write, my name remains anathema in Russia. In late 2019, Russia tried to blame its latest doping scandal on me, ineptly forging messages and emails that no one in the world – even Russian sports officials themselves – found credible. Their actions speak louder than words. The Russian flag will again not fly at the Olympics, this time in Tokyo, because they have been caught cheating yet again, falsifying four years' worth of doping control tests.

I am alone. On very rare occasions, I have been able to send messages to my wife and children, but those opportunities are evaporating. Perhaps someday Veronika could join me in the United States, but that now seems to be a distant possibility.

People ask me if I regret my decision to leave Russia. I do not. I am ferociously competitive, and with my life on the line, I decided to fight my enemies. I have been active in exposing the continuing scandal of doping fraud in Russia, and I will continue to be. In 2018, the US House of Representatives passed the Rodchenkov Anti-Doping Act, which will punish sports cheats and compensate victims of cheating, in international sports competitions across the globe. WADA is hot on the trail of Russian cheating in sport, and I hope to be of assistance.

I am aware that I inhabit a world of apparent contradictions: I am helping the very authorities that I mocked and reviled, to investigate and expose my former associates in Russia.

Yes, the fox has re-entered the henhouse and is expressing concern for the welfare of the hens! I make no apologies for what I did. In the past, I did what I had to do; now I am doing what I *choose* to do. There is a world of difference.

Fleeing Russia was traumatic, but it was worth it and I would do it again. In December 2019, I was honoured to learn that the *Financial Times* had selected me as one of 'Fifty People Who Shaped the Decade'. I was 'the mastermind turned whistle-blower of Russia's massive state-sponsored doping programme'. In the company of such global superstars as Taylor Swift, Mark Zuckerberg and Elon Musk, I was one of only two Russians on the list. Me and Vladimir Putin.

Even though I have spent five years in protective custody, I have chosen not to change my identity and disappear. I will remain Grigory Rodchenkov and will continue to make my voice heard.

In a perfect world, I might start teaching chemistry at an American college and be reunited with my family. I have contributed almost 100 articles to scientific journals as an author or co-author, and I would love to return to my chosen field. As I write this, these goals seem almost unattainable, but who would have predicted that the Berlin Wall would topple in my lifetime, or that the once-omnipotent Soviet Union would cease to exist? Radical changes occur when you least expect them.

I look to the future. This is my story.

GLOSSARY

The world of sport doping has its own distinctive vocabulary. Here is a list of frequently used phrases that you will encounter in this book:

Anabolic steroids have for decades been the most widely used doping substances. They are testosterone-like compounds that increase muscle volume, power and strength in higher doses, and improve endurance and recovery in lower doses. That is why both shot-putters and marathon runners use (and abuse) steroids.

At the elite level, sportsmen and women might use anabolic steroids for 15–30 days and then take a break of 20–30 days, before beginning another session. Such a doping plan, or scheme, is drawn up months before any competition. Only unannounced and out-of-competition testing at training camps, at hotels or at athletes' homes can deter this kind of abuse. The past 15 years have witnessed significant progress in the detection of anabolic steroids: laboratories in Moscow and Cologne in Germany discovered so-called 'long-term metabolites' that are detectable evidence of steroid use.

Previously, such frequently abused anabolics as oxandrolone and Oral Turinabol had been detectable for only about ten days, but that detection window extended to almost five months after the discovery of long-term metabolites. This was a huge victory against doping, because detectability outlasted the effect of the steroid regimen, which meant that many steroids suddenly became useless (though not during the 2014 Winter Olympic Games in Sochi, as you will see).

The most abused steroids are stanozolol (brand names include Stromba and Winstrol), methandienone (brand names include Dianabol, also known as Diana), nandrolone (brand names include Deca-Durabolin in the US and Retabolil in Russia, also known as Deca or Rita), methenolone (brand names include Primobolan, also known as Prima), oxandrolone (brand names include Anavar, also known as Oxana) and dehydrochloromethyltestosterone or DHCMT (brand names include Oral Turinabol, also known as Turik). Of these, stanozolol is the most popular: it is the rare anabolic steroid that can either be injected or ingested as a tablet. One of the first great doping scandals occurred at the 1988 Olympic Games in Seoul, when Canada's Ben Johnson set a world record in the 100 metres, then got busted for stanozolol at doping control.

Stimulants have historically been the most commonly used drugs in sport. You don't often find them used at the elite level, because they are most effective when taken just before competition – when doping control testing is most intense. Some common stimulants, like ephedrines, occur in cold remedies, and methylhexanamine can show up in sports nutrition supplements, which sometimes triggers a positive doping result.

Peptides have become more frequently abused in sport, thanks to progress in biotechnology. Amino acid chains that build muscle mass, they remain difficult to detect because the body metabolises them quickly. The best-known banned peptides are erythropoietin (EPO) and human growth hormone (HGH), which along with synthetic testosterone present big challenges for doping control, because our bodies manufacture those compounds naturally. Direct detection won't tell you much, but there is a relatively new tool to catch cheats – the athlete biological passport (ABP). Updated several times a year, the passport reveals variations in an athlete's *baseline* urine and blood parameters, and highlights abnormal changes that may indicate an anti-doping rule violation (or ADRV, as the World Anti-Doping Agency calls it).

Accredited laboratories test for banned doping substances and their metabolites mostly in urine. By comparison, blood is hard to collect, transport and analyse.

In practice, doping control officers (DCOs) collect urine at training camps, at home and at competitions. Athletes pour their urine into two 'twin' bottles labelled A and B, and then sign a protocol called a doping control form. The twin bottles are delivered to the accredited laboratory, where the analysis is performed. The laboratory opens only the A bottle, to take tiny portions, or aliquots, of it for numerous analytical procedures. The second B bottle remains intact, and is frozen for future analyses.

If the A bottle tests positive for banned substances, the athlete or their representative may request a control analysis of the B bottle. Laboratory personnel then repeat the analysis on the contents of the B bottle, with the athlete or a representative present. In some instances where the authorities suspect an athlete of using a sophisticated doping scheme, or if an Olympic sample is scheduled for later re-testing, the B bottle will be split into two samples, B1 and B2. B2 provides a second backup sample, for future analyses or contested results.

There is a list of the many abbreviations that occur in doping control at the end of the book.

WHO'S WHO

Veronika, Vasily and Marina: My wife, son and daughter.

Dr Vitaly Semenov (1937–2011): My first boss, chief of the doping control laboratory at VNIIFK (the All-Union Scientific and Research Institute for Physical Culture).

Nikolay Parkhomenko (1935–2009): Former world-class wrestler, vice-president of the IWF (International Weightlifting Federation), and Director of the CSP (Centre for the Sports Preparation of the National Teams of Russia). A very powerful person in the history of Russian sport.

Professor Manfred Donike (1933–95): Chief of the Olympic doping control laboratory in Cologne. An incorruptible innovator, and a beloved mentor and close friend of mine who died, as the Russians say, *nyesvoyevremmeno* or 'not in his time', at the age of 62.

Dr Sergey Portugalov: Academic pharmacologist and pre-eminent 'witch doctor,' meaning doping consultant to Russian athletes, until 2014.

Valery Kulichenko: Head coach of the Russian national track and field team, nicknamed 'Pinochet' for his dictatorial demeanour and his habit of always wearing darkened glasses, indoors and out.

Nikita Kamaev: (1963–2016): My childhood friend who became a colleague and collaborator when he ran Russia's Anti-Doping Agency (RUSADA). Died in mysterious circumstances in 2016.

Viktor Chegin: Legendarily successful coach of Russian race walkers, dozens of whom were later disqualified for the abuse of banned substance erythropoietin (EPO) and abnormalities on their athlete biological passports.

Bryan Fogel: Los Angeles filmmaker, competitive cyclist and director of the Academy-Award-winning documentary *Icarus* (2018).

Yuri Nagornykh: Deputy Minister of Sport (2010–16), my direct supervisor before, during and after the Sochi Olympics in 2014.

Natalia Zhelanova, Nagornykh's subordinate in the Ministry of Sport, and 'doping control adviser'.

Evgeny Blokhin: FSB (secret police) agent and leader of the so-called 'plumbers', the men who swapped athletes' test samples at the Sochi Olympics.

Vitaly Mutko: Russian Minister of Sport (2008–16), friend of Putin since the 1990s and the sole survivor of the doping scandal in Sochi. Promoted to Deputy Prime Minister in 2016, he resigned in 2020.

Hajo Seppelt: German filmmaker and journalist, who doggedly reported on international doping scandals and caused me many headaches in 2014 and 2015.

Dick Pound: WADA president from 1999 to 2007. Canadian lawyer and former Olympic swimmer, who chaired the

Independent Commission investigating the widespread doping in Russian track and field.

Richard McLaren: Canadian law professor, who conducted WADA's 'Independent Person' investigation of my revelations concerning cheating at the London and Sochi Olympic Games and sample swapping in our Sochi laboratory.

Vitaly and Yuliya Stepanov: A former RUSADA doping control officer (Vitaly) married to an Olympic runner (Yuliya), they blew the whistle on Russia's doping programme in Hajo Seppelt's 2014 documentary, *The Secrets of Doping: How Russia Makes its Winners*.

PART I

APPRENTICE

CHAPTER 1

THE NEOPHYTE

The year was 1981. I was 22 years old, lying on a sofa in my family's Moscow apartment, with my trousers off. My parents, my sister and I, plus my dog, were squeezed into a 58-square-metre, three-bedroom apartment, considered comfortable living conditions for that time. My mother, an attractive, 54-year-old, dark-haired woman who liked to mention that she had the same proportions as the Venus de Milo, had graduated from the First Moscow State Medical University and finished a surgical residency at a prestigious gynaecological institute. She had been working for decades at the Central Clinical Hospital, better known as the 'Kremlin Hospital', which afforded her access to foreign-made pharmaceuticals.

That day, she had warmed an ampoule of the Hungarian steroid Retabolil in a teacup filled with hot water, before transferring the 50mg dose to a disposable syringe. In 1981, during Leonid Brezhnev's 'period of stagnation', reusable syringes were hard to come by, but not at the Kremlin Hospital.

When the viscous solution became watery, my mother broke the top off the ampoule and drew the contents into the syringe, before plunging the needle into the top of my right buttock. I felt a painful prick, then she tamped the injection site with alcohol.

'Hold that tightly, until the blood stops leaking,' she said, pressing my fingers over her own. 'Lie quietly and don't move.'

To me, an elite runner, the drug felt intoxicating – I could feel energy pouring into my gluteus maximus, the most powerful muscle in a runner's body. As a senior majoring in chemistry at Moscow State University, I had joined the world of sport doping. It would become my life, my career, my joy – and my downfall.

*

How did I end up on that sofa, chemical warmth coursing through my body? Let me go back a little further.

I had asthma as a little boy. My parents lived like almost everyone in the Soviet Union in the late 1950s, during the period known as The Thaw, meaning that they lived in what were challenging conditions, to put it mildly. Joseph Stalin had died and the power of the dreaded secret police had receded somewhat, but the deprivation caused by the Second World War lingered on. After I was born, my parents lived in a damp basement apartment in an old, deteriorating building, which aggravated my breathing problems. While my mother pursued her training as a gynaecological surgeon, my father, a metallurgist, travelled constantly among the filthy, pollution-spewing iron and steel factories that were located far from Moscow.

My parents personified the intellectual schizophrenia necessary for survival in communist Russia. My mother had lost her

My mother Lidia Grigorievna, graduate of the First Moscow
State Medical University, 1952.

own father to one of Stalin's purges; he simply disappeared overnight. My paternal grandfather was one of the millions of Russian
soldiers who perished during the Second World War; he burned
alive in his damaged tank. My mother developed a cautionary
attitude towards authority: be careful, work hard and don't make
too much noise. My father, however, was the opposite: he pointedly never joined the Communist Party, and read Aleksandr
Solzhenitsyn's forbidden novels at home – to the chagrin of my
more orthodox mother.

My father Mikhail Ivanovich, graduate of the Moscow Power
Engineering Institute, 1955.

Once, while we were accompanying him to the famous Zapor-
ozhye steelworks in Ukraine, I was evacuated by train to a
Moscow hospital. Inhalers didn't exist then and steroid treat-
ments were in limited supply. My 'cure' was the same one assigned
to the young Theodore Roosevelt in the mid-nineteenth century –
fresh air and exercise.

While I was growing up, there were only two state television
channels. My father loved to watch hockey or soccer, and my
mother enjoyed figure skating shows and all-star concerts devoted
to Communist Party celebrations. There was nothing on TV for
me, so my mother made sure I was out of the house as much as

possible. School came easily to me. I got good grades, spending just a few minutes each day on homework before going out to play soccer with my friends until dusk. In the wintertime, because our second apartment was at the undeveloped edge of the city, we would escape into the forest and ski until darkness fell or one of our old-fashioned skis broke, whichever came first. I would arrive home wet and icy, drink a pot of tea and plunge underneath my blankets to warm up, sinking into a dreamless sleep.

I first encountered organised sports in ninth grade. My local school, Number 749, had to participate in regular district physical education contests, as part of the mandatory 'Prepared for Work and Defence' programme that was deeply rooted in Soviet history. A coach for the Junior U18 Sport School in my district of Kievsky saw me run an excellent 1,000-metre race, wearing grotty football boots and with no training or strategy whatsoever. He invited me to start training with a group of novice runners, and I loved it. I revelled in the camaraderie among the beginners from different schools – we trained three times a week, staying out until dark and following cross-country ski trails until late autumn, when they started to fill up with snow.

When I was in tenth grade, I ran the fastest 3,000-metre race in the city of Moscow, clocking a time of 8:41.0 indoors. That same year, I also won the 3,000-metre in the prestigious Moscow–Leningrad dual meet and became the Moscow champion in the challenging 5,000-metre run.

I had discovered that I loved competing, and in my worst moments since then, I have drawn from my experience in competitive running. At various times in my life, the Russian and

American governments and the entire sporting world have tried to destroy me. When I've been under pressure, I've remembered the thrill of athletics – how you are paralysed with fear before a big race and feel weak-kneed as you get nearer the stadium.

I'd put on my spikes, take off my tracksuit and see the other runners. I would still be trembling as I stood at the starting line, but the second I heard the starting gun – BANG! – I became a strong and confident fighter. I have vast experience with drugs in sport, but for me, sport *is* the drug, the overwhelming obsession. To compete and admire the excellence of the men and women who devote their lives to achieving the impossible – the seven-foot high jump; the four-minute mile – nothing matters more to me. For me, sport is truth. An occasionally corrupted truth, but a beautiful ideal nonetheless.

Under Soviet and Russian power, and now living in exile, my love for sport has always transcended the difficulties of my situation. I still turn on the television and watch track and field events with the same sense of admiration as I did when I was a teenager. In that sense, I have never grown up.

In the summers, when I wasn't training with the team, I ran through the woods of Moscow's suburbs and along the Krylat-skoe rowing canal with my terrier–husky cross, Ajax.

My asthma became a distant memory. I fell in love with sport, and I have never fallen out of love with it.

*

At high school, my ambition was to attend the prestigious Moscow State University. I aced the entrance exams with 'excellent' marks in mathematics, physics and chemistry, and was admitted to the chemistry department in the autumn of 1977. MSU had the toughest curriculum in the country, and laboratory sessions dragged into the night because we had to clean our labware before we were allowed to go home. Serious athletic training during the academic year was out of the question, but the university sports club had a summer training camp in Estonia, where we ate healthy food, breathed clean air and continued to improve our race times.

Me at the training camp in Estonia, 1980.

During my sophomore year, we hosted a three-way track meeting with Berlin's Humboldt University and the Comenius University in Bratislava. Eyeballing the visiting German and Czech athletes, I couldn't help but notice how powerful the male runners' legs were. Even the women had thick calves and thighs. After I won the 1,500-metre event, a group of us were chatting in the dormitory and the foreign students offered to sell us some Adidas running shoes, which were not available in the USSR. But they didn't want us to pay them with 'soft' roubles, which had no value outside of Russia. They wanted drugs. Anabolic steroids.

As a chemistry major, I knew what steroids were, but I had been conditioned to think of them as stimulants used by American athletes to gain an unfair advantage over our 'clean' Russian men and women. I remember my favourite newspaper, *Sovietsky Sport*, explaining that doping use was common among American athletes, who were switching from amphetamines to muscle-building programmes, fuelled by the systemic use of anabolic steroids. But these visitors hailed from 'friendly socialist' countries rather than the decadent, capitalist world.

Specifically, these runners wanted 50-milligram ampoules of testosterone propionate and five-milligram methandienone pills, which were available in almost any Moscow pharmacy, to increase muscle mass and strength. I had never heard of these drugs and the visitors teased me about being a doping 'virgin', patiently explaining that they wanted the testosterone and methandienone to sell to fellow amateur athletes back home. For themselves, they preferred to inject the anabolic steroid Retabolil, which came in a one-millilitre ampoule containing 50 milligrams of the active ingredient nandrolone decanoate. They injected themselves with Retabolil at the beginning of the training season in late autumn, and when the serious race meetings started, they substituted their doping intake with a different steroid, preferably Oral Turinabol, the so-called 'blue pills' that helped loosen up muscles before competition. Oral Turinabol was purchased from East Germany; this opened up a whole new world to me, and one that I could easily research because our chemistry faculty had one of the best scientific libraries in the USSR.

By coincidence, that was the year that I learned about a real doping scandal rather than the silly innuendo in the Soviet press about US athletes, which was a form of ideological warfare. In 1978, the European Athletic Championships were held in Prague, in socialist Czechoslovakia, and thus broadcast live on Soviet TV – an extremely rare occurrence. A few months later, five discus throwers, shot-putters and a pentathlete from the Eastern Bloc, Russians and Bulgarians, were stripped of their medals after testing positive for nandrolone.

Naturally this news was never announced in Russia, Bulgaria or anywhere else behind the so-called 'Iron Curtain'; I learned about it only because I was in an advanced English language reading group at university, where we read the novels by friend of the proletariat Jack London and the *Morning Star*, the newspaper of the British Communist Party. The final page of the *Star* had an international sport round-up, and I spotted a brief mention of the disqualifications there.

It later transpired that Dr Bernhard Chundela, director of

Prague's comparatively sophisticated doping control laboratory, was working under the thumb of the secret police – not unusual for countries in the Eastern Bloc – and had chosen not to disclose the positive test results during the European games. Members of the European Amateur Athletics Federation's Medical Commission drifted in and out of Chundela's laboratory, but since they were mostly medical doctors, they weren't qualified to interpret the reports from the immunoassay, gas chromatography and mass spectrometry instrumentation.

However, unfortunately for the USSR and for the athletes concerned, Dr Manfred Donike, a chemistry professor from Cologne, was a member of the IAAF Medical Commission. The minute he saw the printouts, he spotted the doping results and raised the alarm. As always, the officials and coaches insisted that the urine or bottles had been contaminated, but the athletes were disqualified for 18 months – a very convenient penalty that would allow them to compete in the forthcoming Moscow Olympic Games in 1980.

Nadezhda Tkachenko was a pentathlete who lost her gold medal in the Prague doping bust, but in the course of her 18-month disqualification she doggedly pursued a 'pharmacology programme', in other words a doping scheme, to prepare for the Moscow Games. At that time there was no out-of-competition doping control; athletes could do whatever they wanted, as long as they tested 'clean' in competition.

Indeed, a 'clean' Tkachenko won a memorable Olympic gold medal in Moscow, recording personal bests in each of the five disciplines in the pentathlon – at the age of 32 and in one day! In the morning, she put the shot 16.84 metres and that evening she ran 800 metres in 2:05.20. Her world record has stood ever since, as the heptathlon replaced the pentathlon as an Olympic event in 1984.

The 1980 Moscow Olympics were a glorious chapter in Soviet history – indeed, people joked that instead of everlasting communism, we had been blessed with the blissful interlude of the Olympics. The city, scrubbed clean for the foreign visitors, was practically deserted; anybody not involved in the Olympics had been packed off to pioneer camps, dachas and government sanatoria. The stores had consumer goods, including salami, Fanta and Marlboro cigarettes. It wasn't the glory of communism, but it was a good start.

In my early twenties, I began to see a dark side to the Soviet sports machine. As an athlete and budding chemist, I became familiar with the steroids, intravenous injections and stimulants competitors were using, and I began to appreciate the sophistication of sport doping regimens. It was like cooking borscht; anyone could assemble the ingredients, but experienced chefs made the best soup.

I discovered scary things. Lev Korobochkin, the doctor responsible for developing new pharmacological schemes during the Moscow Olympics, died suddenly, just two months after the Games, at the age of 49. You can't find anything about his work on the internet; after his death, the repository of his records, including decades' worth of medical analyses and examination data, disappeared from VNIIFK, the All-Union Scientific and Research Institute for Physical Culture, where I would later begin my career as a junior researcher in the doping control laboratory.

*

My own running career was going well, but I couldn't help noticing that some rivals whom I had beaten in the past were starting to run faster times than me. My coach told me that they were probably doping but had no idea what kind of drugs they were using. He told me that I was talented enough to avoid doping use – that I would develop naturally with training, dedication and discipline. I wish he had been right.

My coach belonged to a generation who had competed and trained during the halcyon years of Soviet sport, when propaganda posters declared that 'All World Records Must Belong to Soviet Athletes!' He was the last of an old breed, who thought that hard work and dedication to Marxist–Leninist ideology would push Soviet athletes over the finish line. But times had changed and ideology was yielding to science.

By my senior year, I was showing signs of overtraining. One hot summer day, after an exhausting workout, I spotted blood in my urine and was shocked – I have always remembered the sun illuminating my puddle of urine and seeing what looked like drops of beetroot juice. Before that, my coach had me on a strict diet, which had brought my weight down to 136 pounds. Now I was collapsing in the shower after workouts, drained of energy and floppy-kneed like a drunkard.

At around that time, the head of the university sports club ordered me to participate in two track meets in Czechoslovakia, in Bratislava and Nitra. I was out of shape, but unearthed my spikes from a shelf in my room and started doing some mild circuits, such as ten repetitions of a 500-metre run interrupted by 300-metre jogs, one of my favourite routines. But I felt flat and had no power, no energy and no zest for running. I could taste blood in my mouth, which was a bad sign, but the meet was only three weeks away – as a junior member of the Soviet sports machine, dropping out of a foreign competition was unthinkable. What to do?

My more experienced friends at training camp had explained that three weeks was enough time to start a light course of anabolic steroids: you needed three injections of Retabolil over two weeks, and then an additional week for tuning up muscles and technique. I told myself that three 50-milligram shots wasn't such a big deal, and that sooner or later I'd have to try anabolic steroids just to figure out whether or not they worked for me.

I made the decision by weighing up the two extremes: finding blood in my urine again, or training safely and feeling healthy. My mother supported my decision and told me to be patient while she tracked down some Retabolil.

Working at the Kremlin Hospital made my mother a member of the *nomenklatura* (it comes from the Latin word for 'list,' and there was in fact a list – a long list – of privileged citizens including top ballerinas, writers and scientists, who shopped at special stores and vacationed at special hotels) and gave her access to many difficult-to-obtain consumer goods, such as bananas from 'fraternal' Vietnam or spectacle frames. But all I cared about was the Retabolil ampoules, and the disposable syringes and needles, which is how I ended up on the sofa with a needle sticking out of my buttock.

I began to run twice a day and, as my friends had predicted, felt some soreness in my legs and hips. I wasn't sure whether it was caused by Retabolil or by my longer and more strenuous workouts, but after the third injection my jeans started feeling tight. I had gained about three pounds of muscle.

A few days before taking the train to Bratislava, I set off on a 13-mile evening run in a forest near our apartment. It was chilly, wet and cool, like a typical October evening, except it was still August. Sunny showers, which the Russians call *gribnoy dozhd* or 'mushroom rain', made conditions muddy – not great for running. These were my dog's favourite conditions – dampness, forest pools, and wet grass.

I sped through the 13 miles in an hour and 16 minutes, vaulting over pools and not once slipping in the mud and wet grass. It was easy – just like zooming uphill on a motorcycle. When I finished, I felt fresh enough to do the whole course all over again; meanwhile, poor, dope-free Ajax, my hairy husky-looking dog, collapsed on the wet grass beside me. Just as I would have done, three weeks previously.

On the train to Czechoslovakia, my legs started itching and became stiff. I was worried about cramps, but I needn't have been: I glided through my first training session in Bratislava, and the next day I easily won the 5,000-metre race in just over 14 minutes, an excellent time. Moving on to Nitra, I won the 1,500-metre race, sprinting the final lap well ahead of the rest of the field. As

my prize, I hauled home the heaviest trophy of my career, a large
vase of famous Czech crystal.

*

I graduated from Moscow University in 1982 and, like all young
Soviet men, headed straight into the army, in my case for a three-
month placement with a chemical and biological warfare unit
300 kilometres from Moscow. It was a real army life, in barracks
with no hot water, no mirrors and prehistoric toilets cloaked in a
nausea-inducing miasma. Our boots were so inflexible they felt
like they were made of wood and we were permitted one hot
shower a week, on a Tuesday. We bombed around the local forests
and swamps in military tank trucks that were filled with detoxi-
cants and disinfectants, wearing special hazmat gear and masks;

Soviet Army, 1982. Start of the 400-300-200-100 relay.
I am second from the left.

in theory we were simulating the Soviet response to a chemical warfare attack. When we shed the special gear, we faced our real enemy – swarms of mosquitoes and predatory flies.

The army tried to recruit me as a professional athlete, where my only job would be to train for competitions and bring glory to CSKA, the famous Central Army Sports Club. They even promised to shave a couple of years off my age, in order to guarantee me the benefits of being a 'promising young athlete', but I declined – I loved being a student and saw a future for myself doing laboratory work in chemistry. I was proud of my Moscow University education and had set my sights on a PhD – even life as a penurious graduate student would be better than obeying orders like a dog in the Soviet Army.

I started my graduate studies in a laboratory operating under the wing of the Academician Nikolai Semenov, who had been awarded the 1956 Nobel Prize in Chemistry 'for his research into the mechanism of chemical reactions'. I started to work as an engineer-chemist, attached to a fluorescent and organic dye lasers project in the chemistry department of Moscow University. We were working at the cutting edge of research, and during my first year there we were joined by an attractive young PhD student from the physics department called Veronika. Her speciality was optics and spectroscopy. Mine was chemical kinetics and catalysis.

We collaborated on some projects and started sharing coffee breaks and going for lunch together – you probably know where this is leading. Veronika knew nothing about track and field or why anyone would use anabolic steroids. She sang in the

University Chorus, and they performed in Bulgaria, Yugoslavia and Poland. We had both travelled outside the USSR, which was unusual – very few people our age had ever left the country, and my parents never did either.

We married in June 1983 and honeymooned in the famous Black Sea resort of Sochi. Vegetables there were fresh and abundant, unlike any other place in the USSR. We cooked omelettes, threw together tomato and cucumber salads and boiled chicken with noodles. We had to cook in our tiny apartment because Sochi was extremely expensive and as graduate students, we could not afford restaurants and bars. Our one luxury was the famous satiny *morozhnoye* – ice cream – sold by street vendors.

With Veronika. Celebrating our 25th wedding anniversary,
Cologne, 2008.

In 2007, 24 years later, Sochi would be announced as the host city for the 2014 Winter Olympic Games, which was unimaginable at the time. Mile after mile of sandy beaches, with palm trees waving in the breeze. Who would ever hold a *Winter* Olympics here.

*

I longed to get back into running, but I needed a new coach. One prominent trainer invited me to join his team, on the condition that I participate in his 'pharmacological programme', but it was going to cost me. Stanozolol (Stromba) cost 30 roubles for a bottle of 30 five-milligram pills; Oral Turinabol, or Turik, was ten roubles for one box of 20 pills. A supply that might last several months would cost me 100 roubles, twice the amount of my monthly graduate student stipend!

My steroid habit needed a separate funding scheme, and I had an idea in mind. My friend Stepan had joined the Soviet Army running team in East Germany and was making a living exploiting the price disparities among Russia's socialist allies.

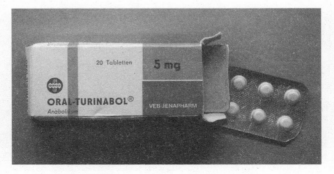

The legendary Oral Turinabol pack of '20 magic blue pills'.

For instance, his wife worked in a restaurant and set aside coffee beans for him, which he resold in East Germany for three times what they cost to buy in Moscow.

One day, while we were running in the forest together, Stepan told me that the ladies in his wife's restaurant were pestering him for Aponeuron, an East German appetite suppressant – they worked around food all day and didn't want to get fat. Stepan liked the pill trade, because transporting tiny blister packs from East Germany was much easier than stuffing his suitcases with Dresden porcelain or the country's famous imitation Levi's jeans. I told him that the same East German pharmacies that were selling him the appetite suppressants, an amphetamine derivative, also sold Turik, our nickname for the famous East German steroid Oral Turinabol. Stepan agreed to buy 50 boxes for me, at 5 roubles each.

I was in business. I sold 45 of the bottles to my coach and teammates for eight roubles each, paid Stepan back and pocketed the 110-rouble profit that I had previously been squandering on steroids, keeping five packs for myself that would last me for the rest of my running career. When I joined the doping control laboratory, I turned out to be the only sports chemist in Moscow who had a specimen of this pharmaceutical steroid preparation – the others in the laboratory only knew it by reputation, even though it was coursing through the bloodstream of many of the most advanced, serious athletes in the country.

By 1985, my career as a semi-professional runner was drawing to a close. Veronika and I had a baby son, Vasily, and I didn't have the time for a serious running programme. We were living in that cramped 58-square-metre apartment (where my mother shot me up with Retabolil), with my parents and my sister. Veronika dreamed of having her own apartment with a kitchen to herself, but that was still several years in the future. For now, she spent the summers with her parents in Saransk, 400 miles from Moscow, which allowed me to travel for competitions and training camps.

My commitment to running became problematic in light of our plans to complete our PhDs. Veronika received hers several years before I did, and at this time her academic stipend was a badly needed source of income for us. I was publishing research, but still had to slog through several more years as a *soiskatel* or applicant before I could catch up with her and earn my doctorate. Veronika and I dreamed of having another child, but our living conditions did not allow it.

Finally, my coach and I agreed to try one last time, but he laid down another condition: that I supplement my steroid intake with pre-race stimulants. Or, to be precise, three doses of Sydnocarb, an old-school Hungarian anti-depressant that has recently been rediscovered by scientists as a possible treatment for Parkinson's disease.

In one of my final races, I ran 1,500 metres in 3:44.5, a personal best. I felt so strong, thanks to the Sydnocarb and stanozolol synergetic power buzzing inside me. I felt twice as powerful as I ever had, and could have run the race all over again, but once I got home I couldn't sleep and went out running just to try to bring myself down.

I was hopelessly over-stimulated, so before my next meet I

took one pill instead of three. That worked fine – I ran 8:02.42, a personal best in a 3,000-metre race, and another PB in the 5,000 metres, 13:52.57, but I wasn't fast enough to qualify for the elite race. The writing was on the wall. 'Enough is enough', as we had learned from Donna Summer, whose songs we first heard on Bulgarian LPs, before they finally appeared in Russia during the *perestroika* years.

In 1985, I was 26 years old, hadn't won any significant trophies or titles and was definitely not an international-calibre runner. I spent several months in training camps; my body was getting stronger, but my dreams of becoming an elite athlete were slipping away. I realised that if I wanted to become an elite sportsman, I would have to completely abandon my family and quit civilised life altogether. The training camps reduced me, intellectually – they didn't exactly encourage the kind of thinking expected from a university graduate. And they also encouraged infantilisation; we behaved like schoolboys and the coach acted like an elementary school teacher.

I'm not sure I realised this at the time, but when I returned to the laboratory I was like an untrained novice – all my scientific thoughts and skills seemed to have evaporated. And then there was the question of doping. My steroid dosage was tiny compared to what the professional runners were taking, but their overdeveloped muscles and prominent veins frightened me. I took anabolics because I was training in harsh conditions, on Moscow's icy or snow-covered roads, in darkness and cold wind. I wasn't in some sunny Black Sea training camp. The athletes there slept for two hours after lunch, but I had to work all day in the laboratory between morning and late-afternoon training sessions.

It felt like torture sometimes, but I tried to keep myself motivated. Doping didn't help me get ahead, but it helped me stay even. At this stage in my life, 'doping was coping', pure and simple.

Anyway, let's not kid ourselves. I wasn't doing anything that other ambitious athletes my age weren't. It wasn't just coaches 'behind the Iron Curtain' who pushed 'pharma programmes' on their charges. Doping may have been a sin for an amateur like myself, but it was a venial one at most. But the USSR didn't have a monopoly on sinning, and my soul wasn't in peril. At least, not yet.

CHAPTER 2

LEARNING THE TRADE

In 1955, an advertisement my mother saw in the *Meditsinskaya Gazeta* newspaper while she was working in a maternity hospital in East Kazakhstan changed her life. It was for a competition for places on the advanced residency training programme at the Moscow Regional Institute of Obstetrics and Gynaecology. She sent in her CV, and she was accepted. She left the provinces and joined the top ranks of Soviet medicine.

A similar thing happened to me. One day in the summer of 1985, I was watching an international soccer game on TV and reading *Sovietsky Sport* when I spotted an announcement at the bottom of the back page: the All-Union Scientific and Research Institute for Physical Culture (VNIIFK) was recruiting staff for its doping control laboratory. They wanted candidates who lived in Moscow, knew chemistry and instrumentation and had a background in physical, organic or analytical chemistry.

I was pretty well versed in those subjects, but had no idea how they might be mobilised to detect doping in a laboratory. I had read about doctors collecting athletes' blood samples and pouring them into test tubes to check for stimulants or steroids, but

I'd never heard of anyone getting caught or punished inside the USSR. Yet there was plenty of evidence of chemical abuse – for example, some female sprinters, runners and jumpers had deep voices, like men, and often displayed similar musculature. That seemed strange. It seemed odd that no one ever got caught and disqualified, and that was why doping control interested me.

I phoned the institute on Monday and found myself talking to Dr Victor Uralets, one of the most accomplished gas chromatographers in the world. Like me, he had graduated from MSU's chemistry faculty, and he knew some of my colleagues in the chemical kinetics laboratory where I was employed.

He politely asked me what kind of work I was looking for, and I explained that I hoped to find a job that would lead to a PhD in analytical or physical chemistry. He invited me to visit the laboratory, where I was surprised to find no blood samples or medical doctors. There were small jars of urine kept in freezers, and some analytical chemists working there. Uralets seemed happy about the prospect of recruiting another MSU graduate for his laboratory. He disappeared into the office of the laboratory chief, Dr Vitaly Semenov, and then invited me in.

Dr Semenov was sitting behind a huge table piled with documents and files. He was in his late forties and balding, but had manipulated his remaining hairs into a comb-over to hide the fact. He sported a small moustache and had sharp dark eyes that seemed to pierce into your thoughts while he was talking to you. I later learned that the girls in the laboratory called him Gypsy because they viewed him as a secretive and shifty character. He told me that the laboratory was launching an important new research and development programme, and they needed staff.

He asked me a few perfunctory questions and hired me on the spot, as a junior researcher reporting to Uralets.

One day I was at university and the next I was a VNIIFK employee, essentially working for Goskomsport, the State Committee for Sports and the Soviet Olympic Committee. This was the kind of change I had been craving: VNIIFK had the latest, Western-made computers and up-to-date analytical instrumentation. The move lifted my spirits and re-kindled my desire to plunge into serious laboratory work.

Dr Uralets gave me copies of foreign journal articles on gas chromatography, mass spectrometry and steroid extraction and analysis to read. While I was perusing such articles on the subway, the police would sometimes ask me to show them what I was reading; *Samizdat*, copies of 'anti-communist' literature often circulated in xerox copies, and copying machines were closely monitored in the USSR. This was 1985 and the tail end of the 'period of stagnation', in a country completely devoid of personal freedoms. The old Soviet Union was literally dying: the sclerotic Communist Party leader Leonid Brezhnev had died in 1982, followed by his equally ancient successor, Yuri Andropov, two years later and then the asthmatic Konstantin Chernenko.

The comparatively young, 54-year-old Mikhail Gorbachev had just taken over as General Secretary of the Communist Party. Once the police saw the English text and the pictures of chromatograms and mass spectra, they would relax and wish me all the best.

Just checking.

I had no idea what to expect in terms of assignments and salary; I figured that I would, at the very least, have access to some sophisticated, American-made computers that I wouldn't find elsewhere in Moscow. That proved to be true. But through some miracle, the International Olympic Committee (IOC) had managed to evade President Ronald Reagan's technology embargo on the 'evil empire' that had been imposed after the 1979 Soviet invasion of Afghanistan.

Just before the 1980 Moscow Olympics – pointedly boycotted by America and its allies – the Belgian Prince Alexandre de Merode, head of the IOC Medical Commission, convinced the Americans to let us import the latest Hewlett-Packard technology necessary for the accreditation of our laboratory. When it looked like we would be sending athletes to Los Angeles for the 1984 Olympics, de Merode secured even more equipment for the Moscow laboratory; no other laboratory in Russia had equipment and computers like ours, and they wouldn't get any until the 1990s, after the 'evil empire' had collapsed.

I loved working in the laboratory at VNIIFK, although I started rattling some cages almost as soon as I arrived. I was amazed to learn that testosterone and the two anabolic steroids that I had been taking for three years, Turik and Stromba, were completely undetectable, even by the latest technology. It seemed totally bizarre that the widely used and abused anabolic steroids were uncontrolled. Moreover, the first Turik sample Semenov's laboratory had ever seen came from my personal stock, collected on the other side of the barricades, as it were. It was the same for Sydnocarb, another staple in the athlete's formulary.

Semenov was not happy to learn this, and told me to clam up. One of the problems with the laboratory, I quickly realised, was that it had no real-life feedback about what to look for. Our senior analysts were PhD scientists in lab coats who had not spent one second in a locker room or on a running track; as a result, they had very little idea which doping drugs athletes were taking, and when they did have a definite target, their expertise lagged behind the athletes' abilities to outwit them. And they were unable to confirm the presence or absence of substances they had never encountered.

Dr Semenov was a unique personality of that time. He was a member of the IOC Medical Commission and had a warm relationship with its chairman, Prince Alexandre de Merode, and with the president of the IOC, Marquis Juan Antonio Samaranch. Semenov's public face proclaimed: My laboratory detects *everything*. That was ridiculous, but all the other anti-doping laboratories were making the same exaggerated claims. The claim of a laboratory in Los Angeles in 1984 that it could detect stanozolol, a steroid widely used among top athletes in the USSR (that we could not detect ourselves), was partly responsible for the Soviet boycott of the LA Games.

＊

There have been two distinct eras in the history of doping control in sport. Between 1967 and 1999, the IOC Medical Commission was in charge. Then, in 1999, the IOC established the World Anti-Doping Agency (WADA), an independent agency created to handle the endless headaches associated with doping control, because the IOC had been losing the war against drugs in sport.

Doping control became inevitable after several cyclists died of apparent drug-related causes during the 1960s. In response, the IOC published a list of banned substances in 1967, but the system was imperfect from the start. At the 1968 Olympics in Mexico City, a Swedish pentathlete was disqualified for drinking a few beers before an event – alcohol was on the list of banned substances!

The IOC's attitude was that doping is evil: drugs could enhance an athlete's performance, but they damaged the player's health. This was not actually true; the athletes' exhausting training regimens harmed them far more than most performance boosters and prompted both athletes and coaches to dream about 'magic pills'; athletes were looking for ways to protect themselves from the physical depredations of Olympic-level preparation. The real purpose of doping is not to build muscles, but rather to help the body recover from competition or survive the rigours of training.

In other words, it was a trade-off: athletes started doping when the potential harm of overtraining exceeded the potential harm of taking drugs. The members of an athlete's entourage – doctors, masseurs and coaches – learned how to use pharmaceutical products and how to avoid problems with doping controls. To be on the safe side, the rules were simple: don't overdose and don't mix too many medications. There was a pharmaceutical revolution in the 1960s, and it presented new opportunities for cheats. The doping control laboratories couldn't keep up.

I understood how this worked. Just a few years before, my summer training sessions had left me weak-kneed, dehydrated, exhausted and peeing blood. They debilitated me far more than the anabolic steroids I started taking to help me recover; ethics aside, I preferred taking the steroids to suffering the gruelling symptoms of overtraining.

To repeat, this wasn't some uniquely 'Soviet' position. Western morality proved to be just as pliable, and American athletes competing in Europe scrupulously observed 'proper preparation' – a euphemism for doping – to enhance their performance. I remember reading Canadian judge Charles Dubin's 657-page 'Inquiry into the Use of Drugs and Banned Practices Intended to Increase Athletic Performance', published after sprinter Ben Johnson tested positive for stanozolol at the 1988 Olympics in Seoul, and being genuinely surprised to read this account in English. It was crazy – Canada operated pretty much like the USSR on the doping front. The inevitable conclusion was that there was no way to win without doping.

Doping has now become a synonym for cheating, which is why in the USSR we always referred to our athletes' 'pharmacology'. As we justified it to ourselves, we were forced to develop schemes and protocols to keep up with our rivals, the blue-tank-top-wearing athletes from East Germany and the United States. Of course they were doping – we had no doubt. Otherwise how could they compete with, or even beat, us Soviet athletes, who had an outstanding background in science, advanced sport medicine and pharmacology, not to mention superb training camps and rigid discipline?

Doping, or cheating, was what our competitors did. Soviet athletes were patriotic, clean and honest, defending the eternal glory of communism. The virtues of doublethink were at work in the world of sport.

In 1985 there were only a few doping control laboratories: Cologne in West Germany, Ghent in Belgium, Kreischa in East Germany, London, Los Angeles, Montreal, Madrid, Moscow, Paris, Prague and Rome. Manfred Donike in Cologne was the unofficial leader of the pack. In 1969 he had invented and synthesised MSTFA, a reagent that could detect small amounts of anabolic steroids, which is still used today. Donike also insisted on accrediting doping control laboratories and harmonising analytical procedures. He established quality control and insisted on airtight record-keeping and documentation, so laboratory analyses could withstand peer review and hold up in court. He lobbied for out-of-competition testing all his life; it finally became a reality at the 1989 World Anti-Doping Conference in Moscow.

In the 1980s, with the creation of WADA still some way off, there were no agreed rules governing the national laboratories, and no shared protocols listing analytical procedures and targeted substances. The Cold War prevented the socialist and capitalist countries from cooperating.

I would remember this lesson for the rest of my life: the doping control laboratories are always behind the dopers, and are mainly factories that churn out false negative results. It didn't take me long to realise that the VNIIFK laboratory was a uniquely Soviet institution. Its primary function was not to catch athletes who were using banned drugs but to instruct the national teams how not to get caught, providing them with details of detection windows and wash-out periods for every anabolic steroid that doctors and coaches were prescribing. The USSR didn't practise doping control per se, but it exerted control over the permitted use of doping substances.

Everybody's 'clean'! Except they aren't.

At the national team level, the ultimate goal was to pass mandatory pre-departure doping control before competing abroad – only those athletes who were certified as 'clean' were allowed to travel outside the Soviet Union. The system was animated by a deep-seated fear of scandal; if a Soviet athlete got busted abroad, numerous Goskomsport apparatchiks would lose their job or their Communist Party membership and with it their foreign trips, the most alluring privilege of Soviet sport.

I knew that inside the Soviet Union, national level track and field athletes used all the steroids and stimulants they could get, without fear of disqualification. Since I had never heard about a Soviet athlete being disqualified inside the USSR, it was clear that doped athletes were safe at home.

Nevertheless, there were rules. Goskomsport apparatchiks chose which athletes would be enrolled in doping programmes; not all of them were allowed in. If you were not enrolled in the programme and got caught doping during a routine in-competition test, you were punished. Besides being barred from profitable trips abroad, you might be excluded from national team training camps or lose access to coveted sporting goods such as the latest Adidas running shoes, which you would never find in a Soviet store.

*

In 1986, Goskomsport and Semenov organised a meeting of the anti-doping subcommittee of the IOC Medical Commission in Moscow. The meeting was held in the Sport Hotel on Leninsky Prospect. The legendary Professor Donike, founder and director of the Institute of Biochemistry of the German Sport University Cologne, chaired the proceedings. He knew and understood sport from the inside, having been a champion cyclist and competed in the Tour de France. He told me that the riders took amphetamines to maintain their competitive spirit and fight fatigue. Later, as director of the Cologne laboratory, he parked his red bike with 'DONIKE' written on the frame at the door to his office.

I remember waiting for Donike with Dr Semenov in the lobby of the hotel. I helped carry his luggage, which seemed to make him feel uncomfortable, and I remember that it was the first time I had seen a suitcase on wheels. Donike was dressed sharply, in a smart tie and a crisp suit. He navigated the world quickly and had a worried face and large, warm eyes.

I introduced myself to Donike, but he had no interest in small talk and promptly asked me what methodology we used for testosterone analysis and how many positives we showed. The question upset me, because we didn't have a detection protocol for testosterone. Semenov was walking right behind us, and although he wasn't fluent in English, he understood what we were talking about. His grimaces were a clear signal that I should change the subject, so we started talking about instrumentation issues. I proudly reported that we had received some fancy new equipment from Hewlett-Packard – an automated gas chromatograph coupled to a mass spectrometer, which would become the gold standard for anti-doping work in years to come.

The next morning, the IOC Medical Commission visited our laboratory, with great pomp and circumstance. All the visitors wore suits and ties, and we laboratory staff wore cleanly pressed lab coats. Our female assistants, who had dolled themselves up, served coffee and snacks. I can still remember the smells of perfume and cigarettes, the tell-tale odours of foreign visitors. Dr Uralets was translating for Dr Semenov, who latched onto Prince Alexandre de Merode like a lamprey, making sure everyone knew the prince was his personal guest.

I was positioned next to our newest Hewlett-Packard instrument and sang its praises like a sales rep. When the visitors left, Donike stayed behind to talk to me, bluntly asking how I detected stanozolol and how many positives we reported. I had anticipated that question, but didn't have a ready answer. I tried to fill the air with technical jargon, to avoid admitting that we had tons of positives. As a junior assistant exchanging information with a top-level foreign investigator, I was in a very precarious position that bordered on insubordination. But Donike kept his hand firmly on the door handle: I was trapped.

'So tell me,' he asked, 'what do you do if you see a positive result?'

'We report it to Dr Semenov, of course.'

'And only to him?'

'Yes.'

'And then what?' Donike came closer, his large eyes making me even more nervous.

'I don't know,' I answered.

What could I say? Donike stared straight at me, hoping that I might add some details to our exchange, but I couldn't. I already felt like a rat. Then he relaxed, and I felt that we had come to some kind of unspoken understanding. He urged me to come to Cologne the following year, to attend his annual workshop in doping analysis.

'Please consider this a personal invitation,' he said. Then he finally left my office, and I was able to breathe again.

Dr Semenov had noticed my private conversation with Donike, and asked what we were talking about. I answered that Professor Donike had inquired about testosterone detection and advised us to purchase another Hewlett-Packard system for that type of analysis.

We did that, but it didn't change much in our war against doping. The athletes quickly learned which anabolics had become detectable and about any increase in the detection windows. The system was perfectly efficient. The moment they or their coaches became aware of any changes in our laboratory practice, they would amend their doping regimens accordingly. We were like field marshals always condemned to fight the previous war.

∗

When I'd started working at VNIIFK in 1985, our testing meth-
odologies might have politely been called 'haphazard'. When our
laboratory was overloaded by samples, Dr Semenov conducted a
triage on what he called 'the catch of the day'. We had to analyse
every sample from track and field athletes and from the weightlifters, who were chronic steroid abusers, and testing swimmers
and cyclists was also a high priority. But when it came to archers,
fencers, gymnasts and figure skaters, Semenov would take the
urine samples and pour them down the sink, before reporting
that 'after all analytical investigations were duly performed, no
prohibited doping substances were found'.

Soccer and hockey enjoyed a special status in the Communist
Party and had their own bespoke testing plans – everyone rooted
for those teams, from the factory floor to the Politburo. Doping
control in hockey was also pretty lax. Sometimes we would receive
urine samples from the national hockey team on Friday evening
and be expected to analyse them immediately. We'd report the
results to Semenov, who handled communications with the
higher-ups obediently and without complaint.

The following story is an example of what our IOC-accredited
laboratory had to contend with. The hammer thrower Yuriy
Sedykh was a two-time Olympic champion, and a huge steroid
abuser. (For the record, Sedykh has denied using sports doping
techniques.) He was just six feet, one inch tall but weighed an
astonishing 243 pounds, almost all of it muscle. He ingested stanozolol in such huge doses that after we had injected his sample
into our Hewlett-Packard machine, an alarm sounded and it
became so contaminated with stanozolol metabolites that the

next few samples spat out false positives, even when we knew there were no steroids present. In laboratory practice, this phenomenon is known as 'memory effect' or 'sample crossover', but we called it the 'Sedykh effect'.

After Sedykh set his world record in Tallinn in 1986, throwing 86.66 metres during a meet between the USSR and East Germany, we received his urine sample in Moscow. It was anonymous, but because it was selected for testing as a world record sample, and because I'd been listening to radio and television reports of his achievement all day, it was easy to join the dots. Even though I diluted his sample with distilled water at a 10:1 ratio, it still overloaded my gas chromatograph mass spectrometer with gigantic peaks of stanozolol metabolites.

The 'Sedykh effect' notwithstanding, we didn't report a positive finding.

Later that year, Sedykh set a world record (which still stands) during the European Athletics Championships in Stuttgart, yet Manfred Donike, who ran the best doping control laboratory in the world, reported nothing. Yuriy must have known what he was doing.

Another high achiever in this category was the talented shot-putter Natalya Lisovskaya, who set an unbelievable world record in Moscow in 1987. She threw the five-kilogram ball 22.60 metres and then beat that new world record in her next attempt, throwing 22.63 metres, another record that still stands.

As I explained to Donike, I reported the results to Semenov, and after that – who knows?

Here is how the story ends: Yuriy Sedykh and Natalya

Lisovskaya later married. They moved to France, where they live with a daughter, and they often speak out against doping in sport. In 2013 they were inducted into the IAAF Hall of Fame, the only couple on the list. Programmed to win, they are shining examples of the close relationship between the state doping programme and the ideology of communism.

CHAPTER 3

BEHIND ENEMY LINES

Working in a doping control laboratory has its quirks. For instance, summer, when most of the domestic and international sporting events take place, is the busy season. As a result, summer vacations were a rarity in my line of work.

After working in the laboratory for three years, I asked Semenov for some time off in the summer of 1988, because Veronika had landed an expenses-paid, three-week-long trip to a sanatorium near Sochi on the Black Sea. Trips like this were a benefit of 'Soviet reality'; if you kept your nose clean and didn't complain about Soviet society, you and your family would be assigned a seaside rental apartment in a Black Sea resort, with all meals provided. The beach functioned as an on-site childcare centre, and street stalls sold fruit and vegetables that were cheaper and better than what you could find in Moscow's perpetually empty grocery stores.

After deliberating for a week or two, Semenov reluctantly approved my trip, but just as I was about to leave, he called me into his office. Looking upset, he confided, while grimacing and pointing his finger upwards, that 'those idiots' at Goskomsport had decided that we needed a top-secret, 'hermetically sealed' laboratory in Seoul during the forthcoming Olympic Games. He assigned me to run it – my vacation had been cut by a third.

A secret laboratory was nothing new – several months before, Semenov had reluctantly helped to set up an unofficial laboratory in a ski chalet in Canmore, where skiing and biathlon events were held during the Winter Olympic Games in Calgary. Unfortunately, Manfred Donike got wind of that scheme, causing a minor scandal.

The Calgary laboratory had its own precedent: incredibly, the Soviets had been planning to hide a doping control laboratory on board a ship in the Port of Los Angeles during the 1984 Olympic Games, after Donike and Don Catlin of UCLA's Olympic Analytical Laboratory announced they would be able to detect all steroids – including stanozolol and testosterone – at the LA Games. Testing athletes before their departure wouldn't suffice – the Soviet sports czars had to have their own on-site laboratory, in order to ensure that no 'dirty' Soviet athletes made it to the starting lines. Remarkably, the secretive Semenov never told his bosses that his own laboratory couldn't detect stanozolol and testosterone.

When Los Angeles wouldn't allow our ship to enter the harbour, that was the last straw. The Politburo pulled the plug and boycotted the Olympics entirely.

The nautical idea resurfaced for the Seoul Games. Semenov instructed me to hide our laboratory instruments aboard the luxury liner *Mikhail Sholokhov*, named for a famous Soviet writer who won the 1965 Nobel Prize. This was an ambitious and reckless idea; from the Soviet point of view, the *Sholokhov* was docking in enemy waters. South Korea was regarded as little more than an American military base masquerading as a country. The last time a Russian ship had docked in Inchon Harbour was in 1905, when the Imperial Japanese navy sank the armoured cruiser *Varyag* after a brief and one-sided battle. It was not an auspicious omen.

Still, we persevered, and equipping the secret laboratory became a military operation. We designed huge wooden boxes to protect and conceal our instruments during their transportation halfway around the world. Our Olympic staging site was in Vladivostok, on the Pacific coast.

As the headquarters for the Pacific Fleet, Vladivostok was a 'closed' city, for which even Soviet citizens needed special permits. When I returned from the Black Sea, I learned that soldiers had loaded our gas chromatograph mass spectrometer onto a military aircraft and flown it across the country. After obtaining a travel permit from my local police station, I hurried to Vladivostok and supervised the boxes' arrival, before arranging for them to be loaded onto the *Sholokhov*.

The liner made one stop, at Busan, where the Olympic sailing events would be held. There, something extraordinary happened. While manoeuvring the yachts inside the hold, an unfortunate sailor was crushed by a heavy metal platform. The crew doctor tried to help him, but the man's injuries were extremely serious and he had neither the experience nor the facilities to treat the victim, whose flesh was turning blue.

By way of a solution, they decided to stash the injured sailor in the ship's freezer. Basically, sailors had no rights. Onboard accidents were kept secret, and the worst secrets were kept in the freezers.

But this was 1988; the more liberal Soviet leader Mikhail Gorbachev was talking about *perestroika* – a 'rebuilding' of Soviet economy and society – and mindsets had begun to change. There was a full complement of Olympic doctors in a makeshift clinic on board the *Sholokhov* – cardiologists, trauma specialists and even a dentist. Breaking with protocol, the crew doctor asked them for help.

When a doctor from Vladivostok saw the patient, he ordered that he be hospitalised immediately. The frightened crew doctor objected, saying we couldn't entrust a Soviet citizen to a hospital run by our country's ideological enemies, but the many singers, artists and musicians on the boat learned of the man's predicament and said they would refuse to perform if a man was dying in the freezer underneath them. When we reached Inchon, a South Korean ambulance pulled up to the ship and whisked the sailor away to one of South Korea's best hospitals. He returned a month later, having made a dramatic recovery.

The incident was a harbinger of a new era in Soviet history; no one could have imagined that the USSR would cease to exist in just three years' time.

For the Soviets, the stakes at Seoul were high and little was left to chance. The major protagonists in the seemingly never-ending Cold War hadn't faced each other at an international sports competition for almost a decade – America boycotted the Moscow Games in 1980, and the Soviets boycotted them right back in Los Angeles in 1984.

The flamboyant American media mogul Ted Turner organised the Goodwill Games in Moscow in 1986, but they were mainly a showcase for Soviet athletes, who crushed the US and East Germany in their total medal count. Doping control analysis at the Goodwill Games turned out to be a formality. Our laboratory uncovered 14 positive results, but apparatchiks from Goskomsport chose not to report them – no one wanted to besmirch Turner's 'alternative Olympics'. Canada's Ben Johnson beat the American Carl Lewis but then tested positive for stanozolol (Stromba).

I did his analysis. The result was never reported.

The embarrassment of a doping disqualification for Soviet athletes at Seoul was out of the question. Semenov explained to me that the Soviet teams had been told to stop taking pills 30 days before travelling to Seoul. Any athlete caught injecting banned substances before the Games would be left in Vladivostok.

Before we left Moscow, I explained to Semenov that it was common for athletes to indulge in an intravenous shot of Stromba or a quick hit of testosterone before a big competition. Our technology would not be able to detect this 'polishing' after a week or two, depending on dosage.

This was not what he wanted to hear. 'Never discuss doping control issues with your bosses,' he said. 'Any time they hear about a problem from you, they will conclude that you are not doing your job properly. If the Goskomsport apparatchiks learn the truth about the problems we have, they will panic. To tell them anything different would be the biggest mistake of your life. Nobody from the Soviet national team is going to have a doping problem at these Games,' he stated. 'And now it's time for you to do your job.'

*

We did do our job, and we had fun doing it. Apart from brief trips to the Cologne laboratory and to Finland, I had never travelled outside the Eastern Bloc for this long, and South Korea felt like an Asian Disneyland. One of the first things we saw in Seoul was a statue of the American general Douglas MacArthur, one of the great anti-communist warriors of the twentieth century – our ideologically prim KGB escorts went crazy when we took a photo of it!

Though they were our supposed adversaries, the South Korean people could not have been friendlier. Whenever we ventured into town, we were surrounded by tiny girls who had been studying Russian with no opportunity to talk to a native speaker. If they understood us, they would practically faint! They had never met a 'real' Russian-speaking person. For them, we were like miraculous apparitions from another planet, and speaking to us was like a challenging but enjoyable final exam.

Not for the first time, our first-hand experience clashed with the cartoons painted by Soviet propaganda. The capitalist South Koreans didn't hate us – they wanted us to buy their cheap electronics, see their schools and taste their exotic barbecue meat. The power of life outside the Iron Curtain to erode political ideology was one reason the USSR limited foreign travel and allowed only 'reliable' functionaries to visit the West. And those reliable functionaries were required to leave a family member at home, just in case.

After Gorbachev came to power in 1985, the rules regarding what was forbidden in Soviet life changed. For instance, my parents had secretly baptised me in the late 1950s, wary of the consequences – that wasn't uncommon, but it wasn't something you advertised. But here in South Korea, when a Methodist minister invited us to visit his church, we accepted with caution. It turned out that TV cameras recorded our presence, but – thankfully – the programme was broadcast on a South Korean religious network that didn't register on the KGB's radar.

Evangelical Christians are very active in South Korea, and almost everywhere we went, people thrust Bibles into our hands. They were Russian-language versions printed in Toronto. It was emblematic of the changed political atmosphere of *perestroika* that everyone brought Bibles home. I had about 20, and the only reaction I got from our KGB minders was, 'Please share them with us.' As part of Gorbachev's wildly unpopular anti-drinking campaign, customs officials had been alerted to watch out for contraband alcohol, and Bibles were suddenly less of a concern. I ended up giving away about ten of the 20 I was given to our security detail, and kept the rest as gifts for my friends back in Moscow.

Even we laboratory personnel had been issued with special uniforms to attend the opening ceremony. It was a rare rainy day, but the dark sky, roaring stadium and international crowd raised the excitement to an impossible level and I remember a crescendo of joy, cheering and even weeping when hundreds of children rushed onto the field in the stadium. When my colleagues asked me what was going on, I pieced together the English translation and realised that these children had been born on 20 September 1981, the day it was announced that Seoul would host the 1988 Olympic Games.

I would be involved with the Olympics for the next quarter-century, but I would have the privilege of attending only two more opening ceremonies: at the Beijing Paralympic Games in 2008 and at the London Olympic Games in 2012.

I followed the Games as closely as I could, and two moments have remained with me. In the anchor leg of the women's 4x400m relay, the USSR's Olga Bryzgina held off two attacks from the greatest female sprinter of all time, the American Florence Griffith Joyner, and set a Soviet world record that stands to this day. 'Flo-Jo', as they called her, also has two world records still in the books.

My other personal highlight was witnessing the Soviet women's unexpected loss to the South Koreans in the gold medal handball final. This was simply unthinkable – our national team had dominated the sport for over a decade. This proved to be among the first signs of cracks in the fabled 'Big Red Machine', the post-war sporting juggernaut that had been the pride and joy of the USSR.

There would soon be no USSR, newly created countries such as Ukraine and Belarus would poach the cream of Soviet athletes and the policies of *glasnost* (openness) and *perestroika* would temporarily topple the massive government sports apparat. Everything was about to change.

*

In terms of illicit doping scandals, Seoul was pretty tame, with just one major bust. Three days after his record-breaking 9.79-second win in the 100 metres, the Canadian sprinter Ben Johnson was disqualified for stanozolol use; his American rival, Carl Lewis, took home the gold medal.

The Johnson bust, I later learned, had been years in the making. South Korean analysts, trained by experts from Donike's laboratory in Cologne, reported the positive result, and Donike himself, as head of the IOC anti-doping subcommittee, reviewed the evidence. He later told me that the entire Canadian delegation, including IOC vice-president and future WADA president Dick Pound, were disappointed at having to announce a positive result. This was not a cut-and-dried case. I saw the test results from the laboratory – the fact was that halfway through the Games, their instrumentation was in desperate need of cleaning and maintenance. The detected peaks of stanozolol metabolites looked a little dubious to me, but it did seem that there was stanozolol in Johnson's sample.

In the end, it was Prince Alexandre de Merode, chairman of the IOC Medical Committee, who made the final call and announced the positive result. It turned out that he was nursing a grievance of his own: not only had he heard rumours about Johnson's doping at the 1986 Goodwill Games, but he was also furious about an incident at the 1984 Los Angeles Games. There, he had been in possession of documents relating to 12 positive drug tests from over 1,500 urine samples, until the entire trove of papers vanished from his presidential suite.

One might ordinarily have suspected some kind of Soviet

'dirty trick', but we had boycotted that Games. De Merode strongly suspected the Americans of organising the theft, possibly with their Canadian allies, and decided to throw the book at Johnson. Bad luck for the maple leaf! After this disqualification he competed again and was busted again, this time for testosterone abuse.

In other news, four athletes from the Eastern Bloc – two Hungarians and two Bulgarians – tested positive for steroids, but they were weightlifters and that kind of behaviour was expected of them. Our team tested 100 per cent 'clean', mainly because of our stringent pre-departure testing protocols. As I boasted to Semenov, 'You can never supersede my results – you can only hope to replicate them.' We had detected several pre-competition positive cases in our laboratory, and, as usual, the worst abusers were the weightlifters and the hammer throwers. But they managed to clean themselves up in the nick of time.

We did have one painful loss because of doping control at Seoul – my childhood friend Yuriy Dumchev, a famous discus thrower. We had become friends at a training camp to prepare for the All-Union School Spartakiada in Lviv in 1976. Yuriy was a talented actor, whose impersonations of cartoon characters, drunken coaches or even of Communist Party General Secretary Leonid Brezhnev would have us in stitches. In 1983 he set a world record in the discus, throwing 71.86 metres.

Yuriy had phoned me before the Seoul Games to ask if the IOC laboratory in South Korea would be able to detect the stimulant Sydnocarb, which I knew well from my running career. Semenov had quizzed me on this very point during the run-up to

Seoul. He knew that Donike represented the gold standard in doping control. I had of course memorised all of Donike's work, and had visited the Cologne laboratory twice, so I was familiar with Donike's testing methods, laboratory instrumentation and personnel. I knew his methodology did not detect Sydnocarb, but Semenov still felt threatened.

'Are you sure that Sydnocarb is undetectable in Cologne?' he kept asking me. 'And is Donike aware of the Sydnocarb issue?'

'Yes to your first question and yes to your second question, too,' I replied.

I remember his short intake of breath. 'What do you mean?' Semenov asked.

'I am afraid there is a small chance, maybe 1 per cent, that Donike could amend his procedures to detect Sydnocarb,' I admitted. 'He might hold that back until the last minute, as an unpleasant surprise for our athletes.'

Semenov was crestfallen – 1 per cent was not a chance he was willing to take. He decided to inform all our national teams that Sydnocarb would be detectable in Seoul, just in case.

So when Yuriy called, I had to tell him to lay off the Sydnocarb; two months before the Games, the USSR had lost its chance of getting a gold medal in the discus. Yuriy competed 'clean' and finished fourth, the absolute worst place in sport – he would never win an Olympic medal in the sport he excelled in. In 1984 he won a useless medal at the 'Friendship Games' in Moscow, Russia's ersatz Olympics event intended to rival the Los Angeles Games.

When I explained to him after the Seoul Games that, for

complicated reasons, Sydnocarb would have been undetectable in Seoul, it broke his heart, but he regrouped and fought to have his 'Friendship Games' award recognised as the equivalent of an Olympic medal. He succeeded and secured a lifetime pension but didn't live to reap the benefits, dying suddenly in Sochi in 2016, at the age of 57.

CHAPTER 4

GLASNOST, OR THINGS FALL APART

In 1988 and 1989, we could feel the earth moving beneath our feet. The world we knew, where newspapers were censored, books were banned and the police made sure you weren't reading illicit material on the subway, was withering away. Gorbachev's policies of *glasnost*, *perestroika* and *uskoryenie* (economic acceleration) seemed promising at first. In 1989, the 'Iron Curtain' and the 'fraternal socialist regimes' of Eastern Europe, such as communist East Germany, Poland and Czechoslovakia, disappeared almost overnight. When citizens of Berlin swarmed over the Berlin Wall, Gorbachev declined to prop up East Germany's dictatorship and most of the communist regimes quickly gave way to quasi-republican forms of democratic government. Totalitarianism was dead – for the moment, at least.

Foreigners cheered what they saw as the advent of civil society and a market-based economy, which was most visible in Moscow and St Petersburg. However, inside Russia, things felt different. The free market was on a rampage, and basic consumer goods

such as bread, butter, vegetables and gasoline were no longer subject to price controls. Before Gorbachev, only the government
owned property in the USSR; now, landlords began to buy or
build apartment buildings and charged whatever rents they could
get away with. Entrepreneurs got rich and we started hearing
about 'oligarchs', fabulously wealthy men – many of them former
Communist Party insiders – who took control of vast sectors of
the economy. For the man or woman on the street, life was becoming more expensive, more difficult and more confusing.

Shortly before the Berlin Wall fell, Dr Uralets and I travelled
to East Germany, which was crumbling in front of our eyes. We
stayed in Dresden, and every night the streets were packed with
demonstrators cheering on the fall of communism. Dr Claus
Clausnitzer, a member of the IOC Medical Commission and director of a laboratory in Kreischa in East Germany, simply
disappeared one day and was never heard from again.

*

Our lives were also affected. On the plus side, after six years of
waiting, my mother was assigned a tiny new two-bedroom apartment in a nice part of Moscow – Krylatskoe, just a mile away from
the rowing canal and the velodrome used in the 1980 Olympics.
While my mother stayed in her old apartment, Veronika, Vasily
and I moved into the new apartment where I would spend the next
23 years. We had a kitchen and bathroom of our own, which was
the stuff of dreams for a young family in the former USSR.

In June 1990 I defended my PhD thesis on the chromato-
graphic and mass spectral detection of synthetic corticosteroids,

and a few days later I contracted tonsillitis. My mother and
Veronika were petrified that I was contagious, which was how I
learned that Veronika was pregnant with our second child. She
was due in December – I was ecstatic.

By the winter of 1990 we had a new-born daughter, and shop-
ping for fresh groceries had become a nightmare. You had to start
queuing an hour before the store opened, in the searing cold. The
most dangerous manoeuvre was squeezing through the narrow
door frame without getting your ribs broken. Food became quite
scarce, with purchases of cheese and butter limited to 500 grams
per visit – if you wanted more, you had to be prepared to queue
for another two hours.

To earn extra money, I took on street-sweeping duties at the
Institute, which was hard work in winter. When it snowed, I had
to arrive two hours early to clear the pavement in front of the
building, working in the dark and with the biting wind tearing
through my clothes. Then I carefully brushed off the stairs to
make sure no one slipped and fell entering the VNIIFK doors. I
would swallow a cup of tea to warm up, and often reported for
work woozy and sleepy, as if I had been drinking something
much stronger.

Semenov was aware of our difficulties and would allow staff
time off during working hours to forage for food in the neigh-
bourhood shops. Sometimes we would stumble across a vegetable
delivery truck selling produce off the back fender, in bulk, with
no weighing and payment in the exact change only. One day, just
before the holidays, Semenov ordered up a veal carcass. We were
chemists rather than butchers, but we somehow divided the spoils

between us. I proudly took home a 25-pound slab of bone and meat, oozing blood, and Veronika hardly knew what to do with it – we didn't have the right tools at home.

Each month, Veronika's mother and father in Mordovia, 650 kilometres south-east of Moscow, would send us a huge parcel bulging with pork, pickled cucumbers, mushrooms, onions, carrots, cabbage, potatoes and honey and I'd use a special collapsible cart to transport the food home. During these initial years of *perestroika*, when the state-run food distribution system more or less collapsed, these carts were in such widespread use that they were banned from the subway during certain hours.

And we were the fortunate ones. When my daughter Marina, just ten weeks old, came down with a nasty infection, my mother arranged for her and my wife to be hospitalised in the Kremlin Hospital, which had plenty of food, a laundry service and adequate heating. At the same time, we sent our seven-year-old son Vasily to Saransk to live with Veronika's parents, where he could at least eat decently.

For the first time in our lives, crime became a genuine concern, and we started staying at the laboratory overnight to protect our valuable instruments, especially computers and printers, from thieves. Marauders stole Dr Uralets's new Lada sedan from the courtyard next to his apartment, and when he contacted the police they simply shrugged their shoulders and told him that it would have been chopped up for parts hours after it disappeared. Uralets was desperate – he belonged to the generation of Soviet true believers, for whom buying a car was a confirmation of success.

By August 1991, the old-line communist *nomenklatura* was fed up with Gorbachev and his reforms, which had plunged the country into near-chaos. There was a coup in Moscow, an unimaginable event for the generations nurtured by Soviet power. A motley coalition of generals and old-line communists 'dismissed' Gorbachev and kept him under house arrest at the Black Sea, where he was on holiday. Faced with popular resistance in Moscow, the coup failed, but it was unclear who would step forward to take over the country.

There were rumours that the army was poised to enter Moscow, and the city felt abandoned. Barricades had sprung up in front of the Russian parliament, and Veronika made me promise not to get involved with the demonstrations. I intended to keep my word, but after being cooped up in the laboratory for two days, I found myself in a bookshop buying five volumes by Aleksandr Solzhenitsyn. (George Orwell's *1984* had likewise appeared in Russia in 1989 for the first time.) Who knew when they might become available again? I made it home that night but couldn't sleep, and when the subway opened at 5.45am, I answered the call emanating from the Echo of Moscow radio station and headed for the 'Russian White House'.

The atmosphere on the steps of parliament was awesome – there was a complete absence of fear and despair and I felt empowered and inspired by the crowd. Nobody asked where I had been on the two previous nights they'd spent outdoors, not knowing if they were going to be attacked, and people accepted me as if I'd been with them the whole time.

After noon, it became clear that the troops were leaving

Moscow – there would be no attack on the parliament. The sun broke through the cloud, and euphoria reigned. We were so happy and relaxed that nobody wanted to go home. I drank vodka from a plastic cup, and shared my precious Dunhill duty-free cigarettes with my new comrades. We wore armbands with the colours of the new Russian flag – red, blue and white. They were upside down, because nobody knew which colour went on top, but nobody cared. Finally, the barricades came down, and the first truck that entered the parliamentary grounds was full of watermelons from Chechnya. I left smoking a Dunhill and feeling faint and dizzy. I believed in the future again.

*

Our laboratory suffered from the domestic turmoil. Dr Uralets received a job offer in the United States and leapt at it; he escaped alone, having spent his last night in my apartment, and then relocated his family to the Nichols Institute in San Diego. This happened a few months before the 1992 Olympic Games in Barcelona, which infuriated the higher-ups at Goskomsport. They accused Semenov of pushing Uralets out, frightened by his competence and qualifications. It was a subtle black mark against Semenov: the perceived elimination of a potential rival.

We were also running short of money. VNIIFK had been split in two and we now worked for the newly created Institute for Sport. The director, Valentin Sych, also ran the Russian Basketball Federation, and one day he delayed our salaries by a month in order that he could pay the national basketball team.

We needed to make money any way we could. Dr Uralets had

The Moscow Laboratory in 1991, from left: Sergey Bolotov, Victor Uralets, me, Vitaly Semenov and Thierry Boghosian from UCLA.

always opposed moonlighting, but after he had left we started to analyse filthy-smelling natural products, such as bear gall bladder, musk deer gland and beaver castoreum, an anal secretion used to make perfume. The deer glands and gall bladders sold well in Asian countries, which believed they enhanced virility. With Russia's borders suddenly open, there was a demand for animal products from Siberia that had previously been embargoed. Foreign customers required certificates of analysis to prove authenticity for almost every product, and our laboratory issued those certificates. We charged a lot of money for what we called 'bile acid profiling' of bears' gall bladders and steroid profiling of musk deer glands, but would stink to high heaven as we travelled home on the subway. Our monthly income tripled, but inflation kept pace.

Another lucrative business opportunity popped up when a huge man who didn't speak Russian showed up one day at the Institute. Looking at his bloated Popeye-like arms, I immediately recognised a steroid user. He claimed to have friends who had suffered injuries, and said that he needed steroids to help them recover. I pointed at his arms and observed that he had some acquaintance with steroids himself.

He didn't disagree and told me he had $200 and needed 20 packs of Diana, or methandienone.

'Do you know Diana?' he asked me and smiled.

'I know her very well,' I answered.

After our initial deal, we agreed on a second pick-up – 100 packs of Diana for $800. A hundred packs cost us $200, so we were doing quite well. This man was apparently part of the security detail at the American Embassy, and we did several deals inside his jacked-up Hummer, which was quite an oddity on the streets of Moscow. Sadly, when he left town he didn't hand our business to his colleagues, so we lost a valuable source of revenue.

Money continued to be a problem, and relations between Sych and Semenov became tense. The Institute was so poor that Sych could no longer afford to pay his driver, so had to learn to drive his brand-new white Lada at an advanced age. Sadly, he was not destined to get much older. In the mid-1990s, he was appointed chief of the Russian Ice Hockey Federation, part of an attempt to turn the national team around after a poor showing at the 1994 Olympics in Lillehammer.

Hockey proved to be as rough a game off the ice as it was on it – in Russia, it was a particularly corrupt sport where it didn't pay to make the wrong enemies. In April 1997, a hitman waiting outside Sych's dacha emptied his Kalashnikov into his car, killing him instantly and badly wounding his wife.

Working under a new regime, Semenov was becoming paranoid, withdrawn and greedy. He was reluctant to share the proceeds from our direct payment arrangements with the power-lifting and synchronised swimming federations, the latter a brand-new organisation. Reluctantly, he parted with small payments of about $100 or $200, at infrequent intervals.

It may be hard to understand how desperate our economic situation was. Yes, we were performing bootleg analyses and selling the doping stuff we were able to get our hands on, but an extra $200 could be the difference between eating decent food and surviving on bread and water for us and our families. Thanks to Mikhail Gorbachev and *perestroika*, some obscure Soviet laws were changed, and so-called 'speculation' – selling and reselling and making profit out of that cycle – was decriminalised. It gave us some ways to receive extra income and survive those times.

One day a man from the Indian Embassy in Moscow came to the Institute. His English was quite technical, and Semenov asked me to translate. The visitor wanted us to analyse out-of-competition urine samples for the Indian national team planning to compete in the 1994 Commonwealth Games, which were to be held in Victoria in Canada. When I escorted him to the door, I learned that he had contracted us to analyse 150 samples at $100 each.

We ended up testing 160 samples, but when my colleague Dr Sergey Bolotov asked Semenov where our money was, Semenov told him that the Indians had never paid. We approached the Indian Embassy, who told us they had indeed paid $16,000, as agreed. That money could buy three new Lada cars, just like Sych's.

When I approached Semenov with two other senior researchers, he got angry and started spinning crazy tales, saying that he couldn't pay us there and then, and that we'd have to wait. But we stood our ground and told him that the laboratory would stop working until we got paid. He became flustered, his face lit up as if he was having a heart attack and he muttered that he would pay us the next day.

The following morning each of us received $2,000 in filthy $100 bills, but when we called the Indian Embassy to complain, they assured us that they had paid Semenov with crisply minted banknotes.

To say that I was ecstatic to receive a job offer from Hewlett-Packard, working in its headquarters in Vienna, would be an understatement. I was looking forward to a life with a steady salary, paid in a currency that people actually wanted, and free from the political chicanery of the sport doping world.

CHAPTER 5

MEET THE WITCH DOCTORS

Between 1994 and 2004 I had several jobs. I spent a few years working for Hewlett-Packard, which eventually merged with Compaq and spun off its analytical products group into a separate company – capitalist *perestroika*! I also had a brief appointment in the former 1988 Olympic laboratory in Calgary, Alberta, which by then had become a centre for toxicology, and spent some time working for an oil and gas company operating in Siberia and the Far East. But the world of sport doping is like obsession and passion; once you are in, you never really leave.

In 1997, Semenov asked me to be his translator at a Lausanne meeting of all the IOC laboratory directors, which had been convened by Prince Alexandre de Merode. We stayed at the five-star Palace Hotel, one of the finest in Europe. It proved to be something of an ambush for Semenov, who found himself in the hot seat during the first group session. His colleagues wanted to know why, as director of an IOC-accredited doping control laboratory, he had failed to share his knowledge of new drugs like bromantane and phenotropyl, which were widely used by Russian athletes. They were especially angry about bromantane, a stimulant originally developed by Soviet scientists to help soldiers and cosmonauts stay awake for days at a time. Numerous findings had been ignored for many years, until several Russian athletes tested positive at the 1996 Olympic Games in Atlanta. Even more spectacularly, Russian athletes had been *selling* bromantane at international competitions.

Russian scientists had developed the newest pharmaceuticals, and Russian athletes had taken it, so why had Semenov never reported its use, or provided bromantane and phenotropyl samples to his colleagues for investigations? His defence was so incoherent that no one could possibly have understood my translation. When he started turning red and became completely disoriented, Prince Alexandre de Merode smiled and stopped the discussion – like a spectator at a bullfight, he didn't need to witness the coup de grace.

After the session the laboratory directors gathered for a meal, and de Merode signalled that all talk about Russian doping was to cease. He invited Semenov to sit next to him, and I sat next to Semenov. As the de facto master of ceremonies, the prince was a stickler for etiquette. He was excessively polite to me, the translator, and smiled indulgently while allowing me to finish eating, before he addressed Semenov.

The following evening, after most of the participants had returned home, Semenov and I dined together in the nearly empty hotel restaurant. I noticed that the table behind us was partially hidden, and reserved for someone special; later that evening, we found out who, when the IOC president, Marquis Juan Antonio Samaranch – the real-life 'Lord of the Olympic Rings' – came over and shook both of Semenov's hands, smiling and indulging in small talk. Semenov would live to fight another day.

*

In 2003, I took a step that would draw me even closer to my previous life.

At the time, prohormones, testosterone-like synthetic steroids, were relatively new, and my friends who were coaches and trainers, always on the lookout for 'magic pills', kept asking me about them. I knew that the best manufacturers in the US were ErgoPharm and Molecular Nutrition and found their Moscow distributor on the internet – Oleg was a former bodybuilder who had become a friend. Now in the sports nutrition business, he offered me a job selling these American steroids in Russia.

Oleg came to my apartment with ten cartons of different kinds of prohormones. He charged me half price and gave me 30 days' worth of credit, a decent offer. I became a kind of super-salesman, peddling expensive Hewlett-Packard instruments, spares and consumables on the one hand, and sports and nutritional supplements on the other. I called my old running buddies who had become coaches, and they were eager to buy my supply, and to reorder more or less at will.

I tried to remind my friends that the most important word in sport doping is 'fear', meaning that users would have to be closely monitored; having administered prohormones for two or three weeks, they had to collect urine samples every few days, bring them to me and pay for the analysis. My former colleagues at the doping control laboratory agreed to test my samples for $50 each, bypassing Semenov completely.

The prohormone business took off like a rocket. We figured out how to combine them with 'classic' anabolics like oxandrolone and methenolone, and then with Oral Turinabol, our old friend Turik, which had become widely available after ten years off the market.

It would have been naïve to think that a serious doping 'supplements' operation like mine and Oleg's could stay under the radar, and it didn't. In March 2003, I received a phone call from Valery Kulichenko, the head coach of the Russian national track and field team. His nickname was 'Pinochet', in tribute to his dictatorial demeanour and habit of wearing sunglasses all the time, even indoors. Kulya, as he was known, was smart, hyperactive and tough. He had grown up in Karaganda, a rough-and-tumble mining city in Kazakhstan, and he knew sport. Before coaching, he had been a 100-metre sprinter and studied medicine in Orenburg, across the Russian border. Sport ran in the family – his wife Valentina was a former world record holder in the 800 metres.

Our booming prohormones business had caught his eye, and he invited me to his office for a talk. Then he laid into me, demanding to know why I hadn't kept him informed of the prohormone avalanche. He made it very clear that national track and field preparation was his turf, and that outsiders were not welcome. I explained that I was merely running a small experiment with some old friends of mine that was winding down, and that I was thinking of taking a job in the petrochemical industry.

Suddenly Kulichenko, probably sensing that I was afraid of him, changed his tune. He started to confide in me like I was an old friend, and complained that his tame 'witch doctor', the shadowy Dr Sergey Portugalov, who enjoyed a professorship sinecure as a VNIIFK researcher, had become secretive and wasn't sharing his doping information with him, while at the same time providing drugs and supplements to the national track and field team. Kulichenko invited me to come over to his house, telling me to 'bring everything you have'.

The Russian and Soviet sports worlds were full of witch doctors, and they also exist in other countries. They are experienced trainers or coaches and some, like Dr Portugalov, have profound medical and scientific knowledge. Sergey was born into an intelligent and well-to-do Moscow family, graduated from a prestigious medical institute and completed a PhD in pharmacology. He was a top-drawer academic who kept himself up-to-date with scientific literature and spoke fluent English. He also wrote the first Russian-language book about sport supplements, nutrition and diet.

The typical witch doctor assembles a coterie of athletes and prescribes a disciplined doping regimen, combined with workouts that change over the course of a preparation cycle. When a competition is a long way off, athletes use heavy doses of steroids to develop their strength or stamina. During pre-competition, they fine-tune their skills and techniques, tapering down to a minimal doping regime. During competition season, athletes become 'clean' and achieve peak condition for major events, like the Olympic Games and World Championships. This is a complicated and sensitive undertaking, and at a higher level it requires an individual approach, and sometimes an idiosyncratic doping plan.

Successful witch doctors try to evade testing protocols imposed by international federations and national testing authorities whenever possible, keeping a close watch on their clients' test samples and substituting clean urine for tainted samples, if possible. In order to succeed, witch doctors need real-time information from experts within doping control laboratories, to keep up with the latest detection wrinkles. They also work with sources inside the testing authorities to anticipate surprise ('no notice') doping control testing. In Russia at that time, all 'surprise' tests were known two months in advance. Witch doctors needed access to an accredited doping laboratory to check urine samples and to test the quality of the pills, capsules and solutions they were selling to their clientele.

Russia is the largest country in the world, with athletes in 11 time zones, and in remote parts of the country, ordinary coaches often become witch doctors. The most prominent example was Viktor Chegin from Saransk, who corrupted an entire generation of race walkers, notorious throughout international competitions for their startling results. Chegin's athletes almost never tested positive for doping during competitions – that's how efficient Russia's pre-departure doping control was.

But once the athlete biological passport was implemented in 2009, it disclosed abnormalities in blood parameters; thus 30 of Chegin's walkers were busted and their results were annulled.

Chegin boasted that he often did as many as 50 injections per day, but his so-called 'education programme' was even worse: he taught 15- and 16-year-old boys and girls to inject erythropoietin (EPO) in hotel toilets and locker rooms. He was utterly reckless; I analysed some of his ampoules over the years, and they often contained fake or tainted medicines. Despite all this, he remains a national legend – he has retained his many decorations and awards, and there is a monument to him in Saransk's central park.

After Chegin, Portugalov ranked a close second. It is no accident, as the Marxists like to say, that he had pretty much cornered the market on bromantane and phenotropyl, using them as a stimulant in his witch's brew of anabolics and the hormone erythropoietin. He offered a one-stop shop for successful athletes in a variety of different sports and he had powerful supporters at Goskomsport, the State Committee for Sports, and its successors, Rossport and the Ministry of Sport. They needed his knowledge and expertise and so watched his back.

*

At that moment, all roads in Russian track and field doping ran through Kulichenko and Portugalov; I knew that if I wanted to survive in the field, I would have to kiss the ring of the country's reigning witch doctor.

I scheduled a meeting with Portugalov. His apartment, where we met, had a comfortable, subdued atmosphere and was lightly scented with the aroma of his Dutch pipe tobacco. Sergey had a broad overview of the Russian doping scene. We agreed that he would be my intermediary with Kulya, and that my role would be to investigate new prohormones for the national team. We also agreed that I could have five top international-level athletes as my personal 'experimental group', a fancy term for guinea pigs. The athletes were desperate, and disappointed with hard-core and 'handful-of-steroid-pills-a-day' schemes, and were eager to try a new approach minimising the use of anabolic steroids. We set to work on the upcoming IAAF World Championships in Paris.

Russia's athletes performed well in Paris in 2003 and won seven gold medals compared with five at the two previous competitions, so Kulya was happy. But the real news was coming out of the United States – the BALCO scandal.

It emerged that the Bay Area Laboratory Co-Operative (BALCO) had been doping athletes with testosterone, growth hormone and EPO for over a decade. Operating under the radar, Victor Conte had built an impressive client list of American athletic superstars, including professional football players, track and field stars and the baseball player Barry Bonds, who still holds the American records for the most home runs both in a single season and during a career. Bonds was indicted and convicted but eventually vindicated on an obstruction of justice charge relating to the US government's BALCO investigation.

Viewed from Russia, it looked a lot like a state-sponsored programme, but it was quite the opposite – capitalism run amok. Conte did not report to the FBI or even the CIA, and he was unable to manipulate the plans of the US Anti-Doping Agency (USADA), the leading testing authority in the USA. But we were curious to know who had been performing doping control analyses for Conte's clientele. A serious doping programme like his always needs backup from an advanced laboratory – who was doing his?

Don Catlin of UCLA's Olympic Analytical Laboratory emerged as something of a hero, announcing that one of Conte's syringes, provided by a whistle-blower, had tested positive for tetrahydrogestrinone (THG), an anabolic steroid sprinkled in the mouth for sublingual and buccal absorption. There was a rush to find urine samples of all the athletes associated with BALCO, but – can you believe it? – a lot of them had vanished. Samples from the 2000 Sydney Olympics or the 1996 Atlanta Olympics, held on American soil? Gone. BALCO exploded one year after the 2002 Winter Olympic Games in Salt Lake City, which was when the IOC decided to preserve urine samples for eight years, in order to anticipate more sophisticated detection methods and advanced instrumentation.

I also learned something from BALCO's methodology. No tablets, pills or capsules! It looked like they used mainly orally administered steroids, and specifically those that were dissolved first before being placed under the tongue, and might be undetectable after a short period of time. This meant that they avoided pills and injections, instead using sublingual applications that were washed around the mouth, or transdermal testosterone that was spread over the skin like a lotion.[1]

Just before the 2004 Summer Olympic Games in Athens, I met another powerful actor on the Russian doping scene, the mysterious and urbane Professor Nikolay Durmanov. He may or

---

1 This knowledge would come in handy before the Sochi Games, in 2014.

may not have been a KGB/FSB colonel, (we could never resolve that one way or the other) and he enjoyed excellent 'trading' (read: erythropoietin (EPO) and human growth hormone (HGH) purchasing) relations with China, where he had once worked. Durmanov was the new medical director of the Russian Olympic Committee, and he resented Portugalov's influence. He was also at war with my old boss, Vitaly Semenov, who remained head of the WADA-accredited laboratory in Moscow, now an independent enterprise called the 'Anti-Doping Centre'. Semenov derided Durmanov as a 'nobody from nowhere', and refused to take his calls, which was not a savvy move.

The good news was that I was now playing in the premier league. Kulichenko, Portugalov and Durmanov sat atop the Mount Olympus dunghill of Russian sport doping, but the air was thin up there and alliances were complex. Portugalov and Durmanov had no use for Semenov, who in turn hated me as an emerging rival for power. At the end of the day, as a well-trained laboratory scientist without a real power base, I had to tread carefully and maintain cordial relations with the warring factions.

Naturally, I cultivated Durmanov and offered him my best advice: lie low until after the Athens Olympic Games in 2004. Once the Games were over, there might be opportunities to reorganise the chaotic sport doping scene. He was extremely well educated, with plenty of experience and a subtle sense of humour. He saw things differently from me, which often gave him a real advantage in our relations.

I explained to him that we were navigating a Bermuda Triangle, with danger around every corner. Portugalov generally controlled the doping supplies for elite athletes and also oversaw the sample collectors, the doping control officers (DCOs). They were corrupt, and substituted urine samples on an extremely large scale. Semenov, meanwhile, ruled his laboratory fiefdom and falsified analyses as and when that was called for.

I planted the seed of an idea: Semenov would have to be replaced. I briefed Portugalov, Kulichenko and Durmanov on the newest doping wrinkles emerging from China, the United States and from Russia. It was too risky to cheat at the collection sites or in the chain of custody process, I argued; to guarantee the success of doping regimes, you needed a competent, iron hand running the laboratory analyses, and that was where I came in. For me to help the doping (and anti-doping) cause, I would have to become director of the Moscow Anti-Doping Centre.

Because I was preparing some of the athletes and consulting with coaches, I wanted to get the latest information from the leading actors on the doping control scene. I wangled an invitation to attend the annual workshop on doping control in Cologne, now named after Manfred Donike, who had died of a heart attack in 1995. Everyone was there, including Dr Costas Georgakopoulos, director of the Olympic laboratory in Athens, boasting about his infallible techno-gimcrackery: latest-generation EPO analysis, high-resolution mass spectrometry (HRMS) to detect tiny amounts of steroid metabolites, carbon isotope ratio mass spectrometry (IRMS) to evaluate the origin of natural-seeming steroids, and new instruments for the detection of human growth hormone (HGH) and prohibited blood transfusions.

It all looked threatening, but I knew how things really

happened at the Olympic Games. There is a vast flow of samples, many of which have to be analysed and reported in 24 hours. Inevitably, some of the analyses are flawed. Moreover, it takes a great deal of time and effort to get an Olympic laboratory pre- pared and accredited, and to train the personnel to work in the presence of foreign observers. Core staff are generally exhausted by the time the Games begin – they just want to go on holiday, which is why the performance of an Olympic laboratory during the Games tends to be below average.

The serious testing happens many years later, when samples can be analysed at leisure. Athens was the first Games where re-testing took place eight years later, in 2012. My 'experimental group' of five guinea pigs produced two golds and two bronze medals in 2004, but in 2012 one of each was stripped away. Reanalysis works – or at least, it does half the time.

That was how things looked from the inside. To the public, WADA was thumping its chest about its success in the anti- doping crusade, with president Dick Pound proclaiming that 'The likelihood of getting caught is getting larger every day.' I remember him spitting out soundbites like 'the message has gone out' and 'the circle is closing around those inclined to cheat' and had to laugh. He talked tough, rather like a loudmouth sheriff from a B-grade Western movie.

As a case in point, WADA bragged that their human growth hormone methodology 'will show if HGH has been in the ath- lete's system up to 84 days before the Olympics'. In actual fact, the methodology was so weak that it could hardly detect huge doses of HGH taken within 24 hours, much less 84 days. After ten years with no improvement, by the time of the Sochi Olympic Games, those HGH tests had been terminated.

Of course, we had the usual headaches with incorrigible athletes in Athens. When the Russian star Irina Korzhanenko won gold in the shot-put, beating her nearest competitor by almost five feet, I called Dr Sergey Portugalov to congratulate him. But a couple of days later, Durmanov phoned me directly from the Athens laboratory and informed me that Korzhanenko's urine sample contained stanozolol. He was sitting next to Don Catlin from Los Angeles and jointly witnessing the positive analysis of her B sample.

There was an explanation, albeit not an excuse. When she underwent pre-departure testing in Moscow, Korzhanenko's body was cool and well hydrated, and the stanozolol metabolites were at an undetectable level. But in the blazing heat of Athens, she became 'warmed and squeezed', and lost water. The heat and her physical exhaustion squeezed her stanozolol deposit (infiltrated into her muscles after injections), which was more than enough to produce urine with detectable levels of metabolites.

The plot thickened. Korzhanenko managed to escape Athens with her gold medal and, having arrived back in Moscow, was threatening to tell the truth about Dr Sergey Portugalov and the national coach Valery Kulichenko to the TV and newspapers. Andrey Mitkov, the popular and hyperactive founder of the All Sports website, had prepared a hall for her press conference, with cameras ready to roll, but Kulya and I convinced her not to show up in Moscow and instead to fly back to her hometown of Rostov. I told her that her revelations wouldn't change anything and Kulya assured her that she would continue to enjoy the perks of an unsullied Olympic champion: a nice apartment, money and a good car.

The promise of no retaliations was our fundamental strategy to prevent dopers from going public about our doping schemes. Irina Korzhanenko cooled down, calculated her personal cost–benefit analysis and agreed to sit tight in Rostov.

Athletes, especially champions, often aren't very smart. Korzhanenko, having won her event, was whooping it up at the finish line and waving the Russian flag for her fans, when she should have been discreetly urinating into a towel inside her running shorts and drinking gallons of water to dilute any doping metabolites that were still in her body. She had done everything she could to get caught, when she had every chance to escape.

The real fallout from Athens related to Vitaly Semenov's job. He had alienated Durmanov and Portugalov, and his 'anti-doping' laboratory would be held responsible for the numerous scandals. The jackals were circling.

Semenov had his ear to the ground, and when Durmanov secretly nominated me to take his place, he went crazy. Previously, in tense turf wars, Semenov had managed to get himself admitted to a hospital for 'stress', a convenient way to avoid his enemies because hospitals were safe zones in Russia – you couldn't be arrested or served with papers there. Semenov wrote paranoid letters to the FSB and the Russian Olympic Committee, insisting that I was a 'WADA agent' (!) who had been placed in Russia to research secret doping programmes and report on 'all state secrets of athletes' preparation'. My mission, according to him, was to destroy Russian sport.

That was his huge mistake – the fact that someone from within Rossport had sent such alarming letters to the FSB, without informing his superiors, reflected badly on them. His boss, the former hockey star Viacheslav 'Slava' Fetisov, understood that Semenov wasn't going to fit into any of Rossport' future plans – he wasn't a team player. And of course, the FSB apparatchiks who received these deranged letters immediately distanced themselves from this madness.

*

Semenov was a goner, not unlike an injured Julius Caesar staggering among his colleagues awaiting the final coup de grace. Fetisov, who had been one of the most famous ice hockey players on earth – he was a two-time Soviet Player of the Year during his years with the CSKA team and winner of two Olympic gold medals and two Stanley Cup championships with the Detroit Red Wings – agreed that I would take over control of the Moscow Anti-Doping Centre.[2]

But firing the wily and well-connected Semenov required a pretext; in the spring of 2005, one presented itself. Four athletes tested positive for anabolic steroids at the National Indoor Athletics Championships in Volgograd. Dr Semenov reported these results to the Centre for the Sports Preparation of the National Teams of Russia (the notorious CSP), directly subordinate to Rossport, but only faxed two of the incriminating results to WADA and the IAAF. The way the system worked meant that

2 How famous was Fetisov? He has an asteroid named after him – 8806 Fetisov.

two of the athletes were 'protected', but it would have been suspicious to report no positive results from such a big event.

Somehow Durmanov found out about both versions – and he made sure WADA did, too. WADA was already quite suspicious of Semenov's laboratory, and discovering two undisclosed positive analyses gave them a pretext to suspend the accreditation of his Moscow laboratory. As a result, all Russian test samples would be sent to foreign laboratories – an unacceptable outcome.

This incident sealed Semenov's fate. On 17 March, Durmanov called me at 10pm, to inform me that Fetisov had signed two directives, effective the next day – one firing Semenov and the other appointing me as the new laboratory director. Everything was kept secret, to prevent Semenov from fleeing to a hospital and feigning illness to avoid the confrontation. Phone calls were to be kept to a minimum. Who knew who was listening?

We had to trap Semenov in the laboratory. Officially, Rossport sent him a memo saying that a foreign delegation was visiting Moscow, and included an 11am visit to the Anti-Doping Centre in their itinerary. A group of Rossport officials showed up at the laboratory. I entered after them and Semenov turned red, as he did when he became upset, glared at me and asked me why I was there, hate and anger in his eyes.

'I am accompanying a foreign delegation as an interpreter,' I answered politely. That seemed plausible, as no one at Rossport spoke English.

Semenov was flabbergasted when Fetisov's directives were read to him. He was ordered to sign both copies of his dismissal – one for him and the other for Rossport files, to con-firm that he was duly notified in front of witnesses.

As planned, I took possession of the official laboratory seal, the symbol of power. We had security guards posted at several doors, just in case – I told him he could spend the weekend as he wished, but that I would return on Monday.

On Monday I changed the locks and codes to all the doors, and made sure a new security team was working at the entrance. At midday I heard the doorbell outside my third-floor suite of offices ringing – it was Semenov, upset that his security pass didn't work. I said that if he had left something, security men would accompany him inside. But he wouldn't be able to use the phones or enter his office – it was my office now.

PART II

MASTER

CHAPTER 1

A QUIET
COUP – *BESPREDEL*

You know what they say: be careful what you wish for. At the age of 46, I had scaled the summit of my profession and was running the WADA-accredited laboratory in Moscow. Our equipment was obsolete and our staff was undisciplined and demoralised by low salaries. I needed to draft in new blood from the chemistry department of Moscow University, my alma mater, and I needed to buy some new equipment from the leading Western manufacturers.

Durmanov, now one rung above me in the pecking order, promised to talk to Fetisov, who committed to purchasing instrumentation that would double our sample throughput. I sent WADA a three-year plan of improvements, and in return received a copy of their International Standard for Laboratories. When WADA's scientific director, Dr Olivier Rabin, told me to 'obey the rules', those were the rules that he was referring to.

Crouched as I was in the starting blocks at my new job, my situation looked secure, but everyone around me was quite jittery.

Durmanov was focused on the upcoming Winter Olympics in Turin. Kulichenko was nervous about the forthcoming IAAF World Championships in Helsinki. The CSP director Nikolay Parkhomenko was perpetually anxious about weightlifters and chain-smoked Marlboros all day. He had plenty to worry about. Russian weightlifting led the way in doping *bespredel* – a situation 'without limits', which meant the rampant and risky abuse of performance-enhancing substances.

*

Let me give you a brief overview of the anti-doping world in which I became a significant player in 2005. Vladimir Putin had been president of the Russian Federation for five years. An avid amateur judo enthusiast, he also loved sport more generally and had lured Fetisov from the New Jersey Devils' front office in 2002 to be the czar of Russian sport. Putin's dream was to host the Olympics, preferably in Moscow. In 2007, he partially achieved that dream, when the IOC awarded the 2014 Winter Games to Sochi, the Black Sea beach resort.

Russia's mediocre medal hauls at the Winter Games in Salt Lake City in 2002 and in Athens in 2004 hung over Fetisov's head. In Athens, around 400 Russian Olympians had passed pre-departure doping control in Moscow, but were caught during the Games. When I replaced Semenov, I promised Fetisov that no Russian athlete pre-tested by my laboratory would be found positive at an Olympic Games. That proved to be true, at five consecutive Games.

WADA was barely five years old, but it was getting its act together. In 2003, the first version of the World Anti-Doping

Code was introduced, followed by a registry of international standards and technical documents. Then WADA launched the online Anti-Doping Administration and Management System (ADAMS), a web-based database for uploading athletes' personal data and locations, the so-called 'whereabouts report' that supposedly helped testing authorities track down athletes any time and any place.

To be brutally honest, WADA staff at that time were naïve about where the doping analyses were coming from. They viewed the national and international sports federations, such as the corrupt International Weightlifting Federation, as the front line in sport doping enforcement, which was absurd. Most of the international federations hated doping control, didn't want to pay for it and viewed the process as an unnecessary headache. Doping control meant scandals, which impacted on a sport's popularity, sponsors, potential attendances and television revenues.

WADA had other vulnerabilities: for one thing, they thought the national doping control laboratories actually wanted to do away with doping. Another mistake was to treat all the accredited laboratories as equal, regardless of the host country's score in the Corruption Perceptions Index, which was published each year by Transparency International. That worked in our favour because it meant that WADA believed that Russian DCOs employed by the Parkhomenko-led CSP worked in the same way that the US Anti-Doping Agency (USADA) did, while they couldn't have been more different. The CSP, and by extension RUSADA, had lists of 'untouchable' athletes, and bribery and urine substitution were not uncommon. WADA assumed that the American laboratory in Salt Lake City and my Moscow Anti-Doping Centre both immediately reported positive results, but in fact the two institutions operated quite differently.

They also assumed that all accredited laboratories were similarly competent, which was not the case. Some WADA-accredited laboratories were just sloppy, and would reach out to other countries' laboratories when they had to process quality control samples to gain re-accreditation.

I have held some unorthodox views about doping that are now considered pure evil, but remember my experience as an elite runner. It is assumed that sport doping is harmful, but the science doesn't bear that out. You might read that a weightlifter died young and was 'a heavy steroid user for years', but if he was overdosing on steroids, he was probably also engaging in an abusive diet and training regimen. A lot of things can kill you, other than sports drugs in lethal doses.

I understand that in some countries there is a stigma associated with using steroids, but that was never the case in Russia. Synthetic steroids have advanced like any other technology – they have become less harmful and more efficient as we have learned which ones to use, how to administer them and what they can accomplish safely.

Training at the Olympic level puts significant strain on the body. Steroids reduce fatigue and trauma, and can also help muscles recover more quickly. I am not aware of any studies concluding that these substances are harmful in moderate dosages, and I know plenty of athletes who used them for years and have lived long and healthy lives.

Let me advance another controversial argument cited by proponents of doping: it brings equality. Some athletes are genetically gifted and can get to the top of their sport with natural training techniques; meanwhile, an athlete who seems unpromising can, after a modest doping regimen, show huge progress in developing skills and stamina, progressing to the point where he or she can challenge visibly stronger rivals. An average athlete might have more room for development and be more dedicated than the 'natural' competitor. I've often seen late bloomers benefit from doping. If sport was 'clean' that would be a reverse handicap, favouring naturally gifted athletes over their less advantaged rivals. Without doping, there is no way to overcome the ability gap.

I disdain the notion of athletes being 'clean'. WADA loves that word, but their mission should really be to protect *honest* athletes. Generally speaking, Soviet and Russian athletes were almost always clean when they had to be, meaning we managed to wash out the evidence of their doping schemes before sending them into competition. They were clean in the same way that a laundered shirt is clean – you wash dirty things to make them clean. When a new methodology was used to reanalyse the urine samples of 'clean' Olympic athletes several years after the Beijing and London Games, hundreds of them were revealed to be dirty.

Laundry and sports have a lot in common.

This isn't a popular line of thinking, but for someone who has spent his life in sports, it is a realistic one.

*

The tenth IAAF World Championships in Helsinki were approaching, and the doping situation, especially the abuse of anabolic steroids and prohormones, was out of control. This was *bespredel* in action: total chaos and lawlessness.

In theory, Russian DCOs conducted surprise out-of-competition testing, but sample collection schedules were known weeks beforehand, so athletes could either make themselves scarce from training camp, or bribe a corrupt DCO and substitute a urine sample. It sounds crazy, but in some training camps, finding clean urine was a problem because so many athletes were dirty! The coaches were drinking gallons of water and emptying their bladders into their athletes' sample bottles. In every batch of 20 samples from a training camp, four usually had the exact same steroid profile, meaning that they came from the same person – generally a coach. My friends who were coaches complained that they didn't have enough urine inside them when DCOs showed up at training camp. Doping control was one of the largest budget line items for the CSP, but it was simply money flushed down the toilet.

The IAAF had its own supposedly sophisticated system for targeting elite Russian athletes, known as the International Registered Testing Pool (IRTP). Athletes in the pool had to enter their travel and training schedules on the ADAMS database three months in advance, to facilitate 'surprise' (called 'no advance notice') testing. A Swedish company, International Doping Test and Management (IDTM), employed the DCOs who collect the samples, but the Russian employees who worked for them were totally corrupt and athletes and coaches generally had two months' notice of 'surprise' testing.

After several months in my new job, I warned Nikolay Durmanov that things were getting out of hand; when he briefed
Fetisov, the former hockey star exploded in anger and summoned
Kulichenko, telling him that if any Russian athletes tested positive at the IAAF World Championships in Helsinki, he would
lose his job. The following day, a florid-faced Kulichenko summoned me to the House on the Embankment and asked me what
to do. I said we had to collect *genuine* urine samples from the
worst offenders, and make sure that they voided immediately
after a training session.

Kulya started collecting real dopers' urine and delivered it to
us in plastic soda bottles. The samples usually contained oxandrolone, Oral Turinabol, methenolone and, less often, traces of
stanozolol. The male athletes were much more disciplined than
the women; some of the girls showed several different anabolics
in their samples. We called them the 'cocktail girls.' (It was crazy
to see Turik [Oral Turinabol], my old friend from my running
years, back in fashion after more than a decade.) This soda bottle
pre-testing worked – the incorrigibles got the message and cleaned
up their act. Russian athletes won seven gold medals in Helsinki,
with no positive result after doping control analysis.

The less good news was that Helsinki was the first championships where the IAAF decided to retain urine samples for eight
years, for possible reanalysis. In 2005, doping control was comparatively weak, but eight years later it was more precise. Our
research discovered long-term metabolites of anabolic steroids,
which was revolutionary: the detection window jumped from
seven days to 70 days, and more. Re-testing of the Russian

athletes who had competed at Helsinki revealed a total of 20 positives: scientific progress had showed that clean urine was actually dirty.

This re-testing triggered a crazy game of time-delayed musical chairs with the Helsinki results. The first wave of reanalyses in 2013 stripped Russia of two medals – Olympic champion Olga Kuzenkova's gold medal in the hammer throwing and Tatyana Kotova's silver in the long jump – but Russia gained a gold when the Belarusian shot-put star Nadezhda Ostapchuk was disqualified and the silver medallist Olga Ryabinkina was promoted.

However, in 2015, a second wave of re-testing exposed 18 more positive results among Russian athletes, including Olga Ryabinkina. Those results got thrown out after an appeal to the Court for Arbitration for Sport (CAS) by Tatyana Andrianova, the bronze medallist in the 800 metres who had tested positive for stanozolol. She argued that the athletes had complied with the WADA rules in 2005 and that the eight-year statute of limitations on the reanalysis of samples had expired. The court agreed with her, and Russia retained most of its medals.

*

In 2007, we ran into some serious trouble, when our two best female hammer throwers, Tatyana Lysenko and Ekaterina Khoroshikh, tested positive after an IAAF event in Doha, Qatar. It took a while for the laboratory in Lausanne to identify metabolites of a new anabolic steroid, with the odd name prohormone (it was Formadrol, 6α-methylandrostenedione), in their urine.

Remarkably, while the laboratory was puzzling over her samples, Tatyana was setting another world record.

Valery Kulichenko was disturbed and summoned me to his apartment, with both women also present and the fateful bottle of Formadrol capsules in the centre of the table. It was the well-known Methyl 1-P brand, produced by Legal Gear in the USA. Together we read a sternly worded letter from Dr Gabriel Dollé, director of the IAAF Medical and Anti-doping Department, reprimanding our athletes. There wasn't going to be any way out of this one.

The women left, and I could tell that Kulichenko knew he had a real scandal on his hands. Lysenko told reporters that she had never taken banned substances and that Kulichenko had sold her the bottle of Formadrol capsules. Valentin Balakhnichev, president of the All-Russian Athletics Federation (ARAF), fired Kulichenko. Then Lysenko's 'coach'-cum-boyfriend-and-car repairman, Nikolay Beloborodov, tried to shake down Kulichenko for $500,000, a sum that he said represented two years of 'lost profits' that would result from her suspension.

In the end, Kulya settled with them and they spent their suspension at the plushest training camps, living like royalty and drawing their full stipends, as if nothing had happened. The only rules of *bespredel* were that there were no rules. Athletes believed they were protected, and they were.

CHAPTER 2

THE AGE OF MIRACLES

On 4 July 2007, the IOC selected Sochi to host the 22nd Winter Olympic Games in 2014. The choice was an eccentric one; Sochi had almost no infrastructure for winter sport, and nowhere near enough hotels for the inevitable hordes of athletes, coaches, media and spectators. The forthcoming seven years yawned ahead of me like an abyss. In Russia, you never knew where you might be twelve months later, let alone seven years. But running an Olympic laboratory would fulfil one of my dreams and would be the greatest accomplishment of my career. I was anxious, frightened and excited, all at the same time.

During the run-up to the 2008 Beijing Olympics, there were some important changes in the hierarchy of Russian sport. Kulichenko had lost his job, while Durmanov, who had successfully managed the doping preparations pipeline from China, vanished into the woodwork. Fetisov, who had been our boss at Rossport, awarded me the coveted Medal for Merit in the Development of Sports and Physical Culture, and left his job to join the Federal Assembly. Rossport became the Ministry of Sport, Tourism and

Youth Policy, and was placed under the command of Vitaly Mutko, the soccer czar of St Petersburg and a long-time ally of Vladimir Putin. At the demand of WADA, a new national anti-doping agency – RUSADA – was established as an autonomous entity. Because RUSADA employed corrupt DCOs to collect urine samples, nothing changed in Russian sport, but its existence placated WADA, which was all that mattered.

The doping lunacy continued apace and I encountered a terrible problem when a famous wrestler and Olympic athlete tested positive for marijuana after the Wrestling World Cup in the Caucasus. I didn't know it was him when I dutifully reported the result to the International Wrestling Federation and WADA – I was working off an anonymised code sheet, and had I known who the wrestler was, I would never have reported him. Some extremely dangerous people controlled Russian wrestling, and I always tried to give them a wide berth.

I was advised in no uncertain terms that I should make the problem go away. Something had to happen to his backup B sample, and something did: his impregnable BEREG-kit sample bottle cracked during the automated opening procedure.

One bottle out of every thousand or so would crack when it was incorrectly inserted into the electronic opening machine. The bottle had to be aligned with the centre of the platform – if it wasn't, it sometimes failed.

We realised that if we put a coin under the bottle after it had been placed on the platform, it would crack. When the wrestler's representative came to the laboratory, I explained to him that we would thaw the frozen urine bottle in warm water and then position a coin in the electronic opening machine. However, we did that, and nothing happened.

We found a bigger coin and the plastic cap cracked, but the glass bottle remained intact. We replaced the plastic cap. Finally, we put a door key under the bottle, and it cracked.

The next day I reported to WADA and the International Wrestling Federation that the B sample analysis had failed for technical reasons, implying that the athlete was cleared. To be safe, I filed a corrective action report (CAR) and drafted a 'root cause analysis', recommending that in the future all B bottles should be opened manually.

Just a few months later, another case occurred. Lada Chernova, a famous Russian javelin thrower who had tested positive for methenolone, came to the laboratory to witness the analysis of her B sample, but while handling her BEREG-kit bottle, she insisted that the sample was not hers and dropped it to the floor. Nothing happened. Then she went out in the corridor and dropped the bottle again, to no effect. I delicately suggested that she try that trick outside the building. God knows what would happen if this crazy javelin thrower started tossing this heavy glass bottle around the laboratory! Then she went out onto the street and repeatedly slammed the bottle against the asphalt pavement, a charade that reminded me of the affair with the wrestler. Still the bottle did not want to crack. I wrote a full report to WADA and to the IAAF, explaining that Chernova's B analysis had been cancelled, and she was disqualified from sport for two years.

*

Another symptom of our national doping *bespredel* was a veritable epidemic of EPO use. At the 2006 European Athletics Championships in Gothenburg, Russian athletes' blood parameters were outrageous. Viktor Chegin, the famous racewalking coach and part-time witch doctor, injected Olga Kaniskina, who won silver in the 20km walk. Her athlete biological passport revealed high haemoglobin and haematocrit counts, betraying EPO use. As a result, the All-Russian Athletics Federation received a letter from Dr Gabriel Dollé that sounded more like a cry for help: please, curb your outrages and be civilised. We see all your tricks! But no one paid any attention.

Before the Beijing Games, Dollé had some suspicions about what Chegin and his race walkers were up to. After a pre-Olympic race-walking qualification event in Cheboksary, he repeatedly asked me to transport the collected urine samples to Lausanne on dry ice, for analysis of EPO. I told him that Russian law forbade sending certain biological fluids abroad; he or the IAAF would need a valid contract with the Ministry of Health.

Thanks to my fast talking, Chegin's merry band lived to fight another day. We had analysed all the samples from Cheboksary and found 18 positives – all EPO and all Russian race walkers. Aleksey Melnikov, the national running coach, swore that Chegin's gang wasn't using EPO, and that I was wrong – we later learned that they had been shooting up with something called 'cardioprotector', which they had purchased from an underground laboratory. Their black-market dealer had assured them that the magic potion contained no EPO – an obvious lie.

But Dr Dollé was like Inspector Javert in *Les Misérables* – he never rested. In late spring 2008, one of our security men called me in my third-floor office to say that there was someone in the lobby who didn't speak Russian, looking for me. It turned out to be a Swedish IDTM employee named Sven Wetter. He had worked all over Europe before falling fell in love, getting married and moving to Athens. He had stopped working for a while, but his DCO credentials were still up-to-date. He had never worked in Russia, and thus had never been caught in the vast net of corruption, which was why Dollé, having finally realised that Russian doping control officers working for IDTM were useless, chose him to collect samples from race walkers in Saransk.

Wetter was low-key and very smart. As a precaution, he had stashed his empty BEREG-kit bottles in a locker at Kazan railway station before coming to our laboratory. He asked me how to get to the race walkers' training camp in Saransk, 650 kilometres east of Moscow, and swore me to secrecy.

Melnikov had lied to me about the race walkers dosing up on EPO and had never produced the promised sample of this magic 'cardioprotector' ampoule, so I was willing to keep a secret. To add insult to injury, he had criticised my chemistry, so I was very happy to help the Wetter gather some samples for the Lausanne laboratory. We'll see who the incompetent chemist is.

I called a local travel agency in Saransk and booked an English-speaking guide for a tour of the city the following day. Then I sorted out train tickets for my guest, we enjoyed a nice dinner and I bade him farewell.

A month later, the bomb exploded. Wetter had smuggled five samples back to Lausanne, and all five race walkers tested positive for EPO. I found it strange that the race walkers voluntarily gave urine samples – did they really believe that they were not doping?

Then Dollé dispatched another Terminator to Saransk, a Ukrainian DCO who spoke Russian. His targets were Olga Kaniskina and Valery Borchin. The Beijing Olympics were just a week away, so this was the optimal time to inject a final dose of EPO. The Ukrainian managed to collect four urine samples, including from Kaniskina and Borchin, but Chegin wasn't going to get burned a second time and activated his own Terminator, an FSB agent who detained the Ukrainian DCO at Bryansk, close to the Russia–Ukraine border.

The DCO crossed the border, but the urine samples did not. They were 'arrested' and kept in a locked room for three days at 90-degree temperatures. They arrived at the laboratory in Moscow in mid-August, accompanied by a letter from the Bryansk customs agents. I telephoned Dollé, but he had already heard the news and closed the case – the chain of custody had been interrupted and the temperature storage parameters violated, so the samples were useless. He told me to destroy the bottles, and I did.

A few days later, both Kaniskina and Borchin won Olympic gold medals in the 20-kilometre walking race. Yet another miracle – it was enough to make you a believer.

Russian athletes performed creditably in Beijing, winning 24 gold medals and finishing third behind China with 51 and the United States with 36. It could have been much worse for us – the Russian Athletic pre-Olympic Championships in Kazan had turned up so many positive results – 99 per cent were anabolic steroids – that it triggered a huge fight with the running boss Melnikov about which athletes should be banned. I argued that it would be highly suspicious if we reported all the samples as negatives, so we targeted a steeplechase runner called Roman Usov for disqualification and let the others slide.

Prior to the championships in Kazan and the Beijing Games, Dollé had travelled to Moscow with a list of 20 athletes who had apparently succeeded in substituting their training camp samples before they were delivered to Lausanne. He struck a deal with Valentin Balakhnichev, the IAAF treasurer who controlled huge payments from the Russian VTB Bank, and who was also president of the All-Russian Athletics Federation: they agreed that no champions from the 2004 Games in Athens would be disqualified, and that no Olympic medals already won would be taken away. However, going forward, things would be different.

Dollé wanted some scalps, and Balakhnichev, who was desperate to keep his position with the IAAF, offered him some – seven, to be precise. Having lost faith in Russian anti-doping tests, Dollé demanded DNA swabs from seven female athletes notorious for tampering with their urine samples for years. It was definitely unethical and illegal – athletes had to be informed why they were being asked to provide DNA samples and provide written consent – but Balakhnichev lied, assuring them that the samples would be used for scientific research and would have no bearing on their competitive status in Beijing. In fact, by taking the tests, the athletes were signing their own death warrant.

Because Russian law at that time prohibited the export of

certain biological fluids, Dollé smuggled the seven test tubes of cotton swabs through customs, allegedly aided by a letter of support signed by Balakhnichev. The whole scandal broke on 30 July. Seven female athletes were barred from Beijing Olympics and disqualified. Then Dollé telephoned me from Beijing to say that the IAAF was deeply concerned about the Russian doping situation, and that I should keep every sample collected at the Kazan championships held earlier that month. That was going to be a big problem for us – there were 100 samples, and a high percentage of them were tainted by steroids.

I tried to buy time by explaining to him that I was busy making arrangements for my mother's funeral (she had sadly died the previous day). I didn't hear from him for two months, so once I had returned from the Paralympic Games in Beijing, I decided to destroy all the Kazan samples. When Dollé finally inquired, I told him that a power failure had caused all our freezers to thaw while I was out of the country. The samples had been spoiled, so we had disposed of them.

He was furious and did not speak to me for a year after that, but he had nothing in writing to prove that he ordered the samples to be retained.

The wily Balakhnichev turned this whole affair to his advantage, explaining to his higher-ups that only his personal contacts and status on the IAAF board had saved the other members of the national team and protected our gold medallists from the 2004 Games. The catastrophe could have been much worse.

*

There was no rest for me after the Beijing Games; I had to start planning for the Sochi Winter Olympics. Most importantly, I needed to build two new state-of-the-art anti-doping laboratories – one in Moscow to replace our antiquated facility, and one in Sochi. I didn't have much time to do this, and I didn't have a viable plan of how to get it done.

Luckily, at a USADA conference in Colorado, I befriended the IOC medical director Dr Patrick Schamasch, a colourful man with an elaborate handlebar moustache, like a retired musketeer. We had a productive meeting that Patrick spent twirling his moustache before advising me to design the Olympic laboratory of my dreams, to think big but remain rational at the same time. We would have to test 2,000 urine samples and 1,000 blood samples over a three-week period. He suggested that I draft a month-by-month plan for each year, leading up to 2014.

I did it. My instinctual graphomania powered me through the planning process, and both Schamasch and WADA's scientific director Olivier Rabin added their imprimatur. I would be running the doping control at Russia's first-ever Winter Olympics; I had my eyes on the prize, and I lunged for it. My profile in Russian sport was rising every day, but I was soon to learn the truth of the Japanese proverb: 'The nail that sticks up shall be hammered down.'

CHAPTER 3

TIME OF TROUBLES

The year 2011 was the worst of my life. The Russian government had launched a new anti-drug police force called the Federal Drug Control Service (FSKN). Its boss was Victor Ivanov, one of Vladimir Putin's old KGB colleagues, an Afghanistan veteran and a militant anti-drug crusader who, in 2010, had travelled to California to lobby against a referendum that proposed to legalise marijuana. (!) The measure failed.

Russia, like many First and Second World countries, had a significant drug problem. Veterans of the war in Afghanistan had introduced heroin onto the streets of many cities, and Russian kids had access to all manner of licit and illicit drugs. But the FSKN didn't target me as part of its war on drugs; rather, they were eager to corner the lucrative market in anabolic steroids and sports nutrition supplements, and I was a thorn in their side. I had been alerting athletes to the mislabelling of various FSKN-endorsed products and kept scrupulous records of high-quality supplements, which I shared with elite athletes.

The real money in the steroid and supplement marketplace came from sales to amateur athletes, policemen, bodybuilders and gym rats who wanted the compounds that the 'real' athletes were using. This market was driven by internet sales, and many websites were using my information to promote their products: for example, 'Highest quality supplements, assured by Dr Grigory Rodchenkov, chief of Russia's national sport testing laboratory,' and so on.

Remember: The raised nail must be hammered down.

I was also in the process of building two new four-storey, state-of-the art doping control laboratories, and the FSKN coveted both facilities for locations. If they could put me out of business, they could take over both the legitimate and the black market doping control business in Russia and no one would be able to challenge their credibility or their power.

Why did they attack me? Because they could. The Anti-Doping Centre and I enjoyed the protection of the remaining pre-Putin cadres in the FSB, but Ivanov and Co. represented new blood, with new loyalties. I was about to become a victim of a turf war between rival factions of the secret police.

My trouble started at 7pm on Friday 11 February 2011, just as I was getting ready to leave work and go home. I planned to fly to Germany the next day, to present some of our recent research into long-term metabolites of popular anabolic steroids like Oral Turinabol and oxandrolone at the Manfred Donike Workshop in Cologne. Suddenly, several FSKN investigators and about ten black-uniformed special assignment policemen in balaclavas burst into our third-floor laboratory. They searched my office, seized my collection of prohormones and steroids and escorted me to the Moscow headquarters of the FSKN, on Azovskaya Street.

They questioned me for the whole night, confiscating both my cell phones. At the same time, they were also searching my sister Marina's apartment and hauling her to Azovskaya Street for a night of questioning. Marina was a successful track and field athlete and coach, and they knew that persecuting her would exert more pressure on me.

After my all-night interrogation, I signed several pages of investigative protocols admitting some fairly serious charges, including steroid trafficking and distribution, in collusion with my sister. I was fingerprinted and released at around 7am. I smoked a couple of cigarettes with the FSKN officers and drove home in the dark, without my phones and crazy with fear and lack of sleep. Veronika hadn't slept either, but we rushed to the airport and flew to Germany. I couldn't concentrate on anything at the workshop – I could barely muster the will to eat or drink – and I spent most of the time Skyping friends in Moscow, who suggested that I might be arrested at the airport on my return and told me to hire an experienced lawyer.

My friends were right: as soon as we'd passed through passport control on our return, the FSKN police grabbed me and took me to their downtown headquarters for further questioning. This time my lawyer was present, and we declared that all my previous statements had been made under duress and withdrew the declarations I had made during the night of 11 February. Russian law prohibited administrative detentions and questioning between the hours of 10pm and 6am, precisely the time the FSKN agents were working me over – this would prove immensely helpful.

This infuriated them even more and they ratcheted up their

threats, informing me I was no longer a suspect but an accused criminal – I was not to leave Moscow. I would be allowed to go to work and to return home, but nothing more.

They then turned my tiny, 38-square-metre apartment upside down and spent all night searching it. Veronika watched the catastrophe unfold. I was completely wasted when they finally left around 5am. I slept for a couple of hours and then headed back to the laboratory.

The next day they showed up at my office and the process began all over again. They examined every shelf, opened every drawer, vetted every file and seized my computer. They seemed happy to find a 15-year-old ampoule of stanozolol. I was terrified and my nerves were completely shot.

The FSKN ordered me to appear at their offices for a final confrontation, on 24 February, the day after Russian Army Day. They strongly advised me to plead guilty to their trumped-up charges and to restate the admissions I'd made during the all-night interrogation at Azovskaya Street. They also expected me to testify against my sister; if I did so, they offered to treat me as a cooperating witness and to dismiss the criminal complaints against me, resolving all my problems. They would go ahead and prosecute Marina, but because she had a two-year-old daughter, she'd get a year or two of probation instead of prison.

Those are our terms, they said – reject them at your peril.

I rejected them. I knew my history of Bolshevik and Stalinist investigations, so I knew they had no intention of keeping their word. Stalinism, the era of torture-induced 'confessions', followed by lengthy prison terms or worse, wasn't so far in the past.

My FSKN tormentors told me to reconsider, explaining that if I didn't, they would arrest me and throw me in prison. They had pushed me beyond my limits. I didn't think I could physically survive any more interrogations; I did not foresee that these horrors would last for almost a year and a half.

I'd never been in a situation like this and thought another interrogation would break me. I never celebrated Russian Army Day, but I felt so awful that I uncorked a bottle of White Horse whisky that had been gathering dust in my kitchen for years. I had downed about five ounces, and felt nothing, when suddenly an idea clicked in my mind. I realised that there was no way I could return to the FSKN office the next day and face arrest. I decided to kill myself.

It was as if someone had flipped a switch from 'Life' to 'Death' mode. I was on autopilot and felt drained of emotion. I wasn't trembling, I wasn't balancing the pros and cons in my mind and I wasn't suffering. My death became inevitable; there was no turning back.

If I'd owned a pistol, I would have shot myself. Instead, I plunged a kitchen knife into my heart while lying in the bathtub and saw blood bubbling out of my chest and snaking like a crimson silk scarf in the water around me.

Luckily, Veronika had sensed that I might do something desperate, and was keeping track of my whereabouts in our tiny apartment. She called an ambulance, and because it was a state holiday, there were very few cars on the roads. Within 20 minutes, we pulled up at the famous Sklifosovsky Emergency Hospital. Drunkards always tended to cut each other up on public holidays, so one of Moscow's greatest cardiac surgeons, Dr Elena Lebedeva, was on duty.

As I lay on the hospital trolley, I could see almost no blood flowing out of my chest wound – I had been lucky and the knife had cut into the right chamber of my heart. Had I stabbed myself just an inch to the left, or even at a slightly different angle, I would have penetrated the left chamber, which pumps blood away from the heart, and a fountain of blood would have flooded into my lungs. I was fully conscious and felt quite relaxed until they put me under. Then I remember nothing but darkness.

When I opened my eyes the next day, I was lying in a large sunlit room. (Not heaven!) The two nurses standing next to the bed looked down at me and murmured, 'Look – he's alive.' They had immobilised me with tightly wrapped towels. A drainage tube stuck out between my ribs, channelling away blood and other liquid that had collected in my lungs during the surgery.

I spent the next week in the small psychiatric wing at the Sklifosovsky Hospital and was placed on suicide watch. For several days, my hands were tightly bound to prevent any attempt on my own life. After a psychiatric examination and a visit from Veronika, they unbound me so I could sit freely and eat with my own hands, and the catheter was removed from my penis. The switch had flipped back to 'Life' mode and I did not want to repeat the suicide attempt. Of course, the hospital took the required precautions, feeding me all kinds of pills and injecting me twice a day. I assume I was being tranquillised, but I don't know for sure.

I was as happy as I have ever been – I felt as if I had received a gift from God. Doctor Lebedeva had saved my life.

After a week, the nurses removed the drainage tube from my side, which allowed me to walk around the ward more freely. The psychiatric wing of the hospital was packed, and the police kept a constant watch over some of the patients. Those of us who were allowed to roam the corridors became friends. They turned out to be failed suicides for the most part – men who had tried to slit their wrists or who had swallowed a handful of three-inch nails, a method that was apparently quite common.

One man, a truck driver, had an astonishing story. His wife disappeared, and her murdered corpse was found 50 miles away from their home. The police immediately arrested him and tried to force him to confess to the homicide. He refused – he had cell phone location data that showed that he had been driving his truck all day and night, in a different part of the country – but the police were lazy. They didn't want to investigate the crime, and if they could coerce him to confess, they could close the case.

After arresting him, the police took him to his garage to search his truck for blood spots or any other evidence linking him to the crime. During the search, he managed to grab a knife from under the driver's seat, and committed *seppuku* – Japanese hara-kiri – cutting so deeply into his belly that his guts were ready to fall out. The police rushed him to the Sklifosovsky Hospital, where surgeons saved his life.

He was still very weak, and the police kept a close eye on him as the two of us shuffled back and forth along the hospital corridor.

Others were less fortunate. There were a couple of men who had thrown themselves off a roof or through a window, and succeeded only in breaking their backs. They watched us wistfully as we walked around the ward, their eyes full of tears.

The FSKN agents wanted to interrogate me inside the tiny psych ward, but my lawyer and my doctor held them at bay. I was released on 13 March and the next day went to meet Patrick Schamasch, who was overseeing our preparations for the 2014 Sochi Olympics. I was taking all kinds of pills to stabilise my mood that made me drowsy and unfocused and Schamasch gazed at me a few times as we sat in the conference room. I'm sure he had a good idea of what was wrong with me, but he wasn't looking to make trouble for me or for the Olympic satellite laboratory in Sochi, which would be a temporary clone of the Moscow Anti-Doping Centre.

The next day, the FSKN hauled me in for several more hours of questioning. They jumped from one topic to another, trying to disorient me and hinting that they had witness statements to suggest that I had been 'selling' steroids, when in fact having them in my possession and giving them to athletes was a required part of my job with the laboratory. I asked for the witnesses' names but they declined to tell me. From their questions it became clear that they had been tapping my phones for the last two years, and that they had also hacked into my email accounts.

Another torture for me was reading the summary of my interrogation. My most successful answers had been rephrased in sloppy wording, as if I had been drunk or unconscious when I gave them. I checked every word and phrase and then my lawyer did the same. Then the furious investigator made some changes, printed out a new version and we continued proofreading. In the final version, I carefully filled in any lines or margins where the FSKN might add other words and phrases in order to falsify the document.

By the end of the day, I was morally and physically exhausted. The after-effects of the surgery and the pills swirling around my brain were disorienting me and my mental condition was getting worse each day, especially at night-time. Feverish dreams interrupted my sleep and I woke up dizzy and overwhelmed. I decided to stop taking my pills: I was paranoid and thought the doctors were deliberately poisoning me, in order to render me unable to fulfil my duties as ADC director.

Kicking the pills was a risky experiment. Veronika and my friends felt they couldn't leave me without medical care, so I decided to check myself in to a local psychiatric clinic on an emergency basis, claiming an inability to cope with daily life. The emergency psychiatric ambulance arrived at our building, and the doctors who interviewed me couldn't figure out if it was worth institutionalising me, but agreed when I strongly insisted. I told them that I couldn't spend one more night in my apartment after the vicious search performed by the FSKN investigators and was being frightened by my dreams.

It turned out to be a good choice. I landed in a decent hospital catering to Moscow residents, and by the end of my five-week stay I felt much better. A gaggle of incompetent 70-year-old female psychiatrists, who seemed to me like functioning schizophrenics, conducted my exit examination, which was like talking to aliens. When I told them about our pioneering investigations on steroid analysis, using the newest instrumentation, they asked me who did that, in which country and where I had read about it. I replied that this was happening at that very moment, in my laboratory in Moscow, and they thought I was nuts.

After a lengthy interview, they determined that my mental state was 'inconclusive' (whatever that meant), and that I entertained the delusion that I was a prominent person. They grudgingly released me in late April.

The FSKN wasn't done with me and wanted to recommit me to a psychiatric facility. I refused, so they sued me in the notoriously pro-government Basmanny District Court, famous for dispensing fake justice. The judge never bothered to read your pleas or listen to your defence lawyers. The prosecutors and FSKN types sat across from me, confident that all decisions would be decided in their favour – which they were. They had provided the court with the desired decision on a USB stick, the day before. They printed out and signed the five-page Court Award in five minutes.

Predictably, the court sentenced me to a full examination at the famous Alekseev Psychiatric Clinic, also known as 'Kashchenko', a hundred-year-old institution often mentioned in jokes and folk songs. The 'white realm of hidden faces', according to the poet Joseph Brodsky, an earlier visitor.

The time in Kashchenko actually worked out well for me. If you were a criminal or severely disturbed, they knew how to handle you, but they quickly realised that I was a fully functioning member of society and treated me accordingly. After I had been there a week, they began to let me use a computer for an hour each day after lunch, so I could conduct business and answer emails as if I were at work in my office. This was important and morale-building, because July was always busy with important sporting events and there were tons of urine samples to be analysed and reported. I was happy to be working again, just as if I were sitting in my office.

I suddenly realised that the FSKN's vice-like jaws hadn't choked the life out of me, that I could breathe freely and work freely. I felt hopeful and optimistic. After a thorough investigation, the psychiatrists released me after three weeks, having confirmed that the FSKN's all-night interview had caused my psychiatric stress and that any statements I'd made that night were null and void. They gave me a provisional clean bill of mental health.

My lawyer and I were happy. I felt stronger and for the first time in months, I dreamed of surviving this ordeal and defeating the FSKN. Their investigators were furious, of course. They wanted to break me and destroy me professionally, and I hated everyone from that organisation in return.

*

Curiously, I managed to get a fair amount of work done while the FSKN was making my life miserable. The newly appointed Deputy Minister for Sport, Yuri Nagornykh, put me in touch with the FSB officer Evgeny Blokhin, who would be attached to the ADC. This in itself was not so unusual; KGB and FSB 'minders' were not uncommon in sport, especially among athletes or officials who had frequent contact with foreigners. Unbeknownst to me, Blokhin was going to play a crucial role in the preparation for the Sochi Games.

This secret policeman was in his early thirties and had a very bland appearance. His behaviour was so nondescript that you would not have remembered anything about him if you met him in a train, bar or store. He shared this trait of forgettability with his one-time boss, the former KGB director Vladimir Putin. There is a famous biography of Putin entitled *The Man Without a Face*. I later realised that his assignment was to avoid leaving any traces of the greatest fraud in the sport's history – the Sochi Games in 2014.

Blokhin was assigned to RUSADA, and to my Anti-Doping Centre. He and I examined the blueprints for the Sochi Olympic Laboratory, and he instructed me to reserve two rooms for FSB agents. He explained that every Olympic venue in Sochi had such rooms, so we assigned two rooms on the fourth floor of the laboratory.

Because I was running out of creative names for the many rooms in our laboratory, I inscribed the capital letters right onto the blueprint: 'FSB'. The drawings sailed through the bureaucracy, but when Blokhin saw the final, pre-construction plans, he blew up when he saw those letters on them and made sure I got the project manager to erase them before we proceeded any further.

It was right around the time Blokhin entered our lives that I discovered the cocktail. Steroid detection had become so sophisticated that we had to wean athletes off pills and injections, and we realised that if you consumed steroids dissolved in alcohol by swirling the mixture around in your mouth, the most risky, or detectable, long-term metabolites would not emerge. I'd remembered one important detail from the BALCO scandal: they never used pills. Buccal absorption – letting pills dissolve in your mouth – or transdermal lotion were the only low-risk and, hopefully, efficient ways to administer steroids.

I dreamed up the cocktail in my mind, a combination of methenolone, trenbolone and oxandrolone, dissolved in Chivas Regal whisky, and then mixed it up in my kitchen. Some athletes found the whisky too bitter, so my assistants, who learned how to prepare the cocktail (my lawyer and the centre's FSB handlers didn't want me to experiment with steroids during the FSKN investigation), created a new version of the cocktail using vermouth. Irina Rodionova, a medical doctor who had followed Nagornykh to the the Ministry of Sport, Tourism and Youth Policy, christened the cocktail the 'Duchess' after her favourite yellow, pear-flavoured lemonade that we drank from heavy glass bottles as children in the 1960s.

At the end of this productive summer, the FSKN attacked me again. They needed to overturn the conclusions of the Kashchenko psychiatrists, so they went back to the Basmanny District Court and surprise, surprise, the judge accepted their motion, printing his decision off a USB stick handed to him by one of the prosecutors. If only George Orwell had been alive to chronicle this dark parody of justice.

The judge ordered me to be institutionalised for another four weeks, this time at the State Scientific Centre for Social and Forensic Psychiatry, better known as the Serbsky Institute. A clinic specialising in forensic psychiatry, the Serbsky had a dark history as an instrument of oppression for the Soviet regime, and now for Putin's government. Dissidents such as Vladimir Bukovsky, the serial killer Andrei Chikatilo and General Peter Grigorenko were 'analysed' at the Serbsky before being sent into exile abroad, shot and imprisoned, respectively. I wasn't sure I could survive it, but I was ready to fight.

Luckily my lawyer noticed that the court had forgotten to specify a time period for my commitment, so I continued working as director of the Anti-Doping Centre. In November, one of the senior FSKN investigators, a female colonel, finally said she was sending police officers to take me to the Serbsky Institute. My lawyer immediately checked me in to a cardiac sanatorium in the Moscow suburbs, arguing that the threats from the FSKN had affected my health.

Then we solved the puzzle. Vacancies were quite rare at the Serbsky, with patients seeking admission from all over Russia. When a bed became available, the FSKN became hyperactive in their efforts to commit me, so we started monitoring the admissions situation ourselves. The Serbsky went months without having a free bed, but places tended to open up following the New Year holiday, so I headed for the sanatorium in early January. When we knew the wards had filled up again, I returned to Moscow and resumed my work.

The only joy was our new dog, a Pomeranian named Vrangel. He was smart, playful and exuded an infectious optimism. He relaxed me so much that my life started to seem almost bearable. Vrangel was a strange name for a dog – General Peter Vrangel was a ferocious 'enemy of the Revolution' who led an anti-communist army against the Bolsheviks during the Civil War of 1918–21.

General Vrangel organised a famous evacuation of the Crimea in the face of the oncoming Bolshevik 'Red' Army, after the Bolsheviks had promised amnesty to any 'Whites' who surrendered. Vrangel fled, and arranged to ferry 145,000 soldiers and civilians to foreign ports; 50,000 Whites chose to remain, and were executed by the Bolsheviks in one of the Revolution's many Red Terrors. Like Vrangel, I didn't trust the word of the FSKN, the police or Vladimir Putin.

By the way, George Orwell also had a dog, named Marx. Karl Marx.

*

The Olympic year of 2012 proved to be decisive in my fight with FSKN. In March, WADA organised a meeting of all its laboratory directors, including me, in London, followed by a tour of the new Olympic laboratory in Harlow, ten miles outside London. The meeting was preceded by the Manfred Donike Workshop in Cologne, so I booked flights from Cologne to London. I applied for a UK and a Schengen visa, and kept the deputy minister Nagornykh apprised of my plans. He supported me, and we wrote a letter to the FSKN explaining that my visit to London was of the highest strategic importance and would provide a unique source of information about doping control during the Olympic Games. The FSKN didn't answer, but nor did they turn me down. *'Molchanie znak soglasiya,'* as the old Russian proverb goes. 'Silence is a sign of assent.'

We re-sent the letter in duplicate: an official-looking messenger called a *Feldjäger*, with a uniform and a sidearm, delivered one copy, and we had the other deposited at the FSKN's central reception, requiring written confirmation of receipt. Astonishingly, this worked, and on 15 February the FSKN General Nerses Mirzoyants summoned me to his office for a meeting.

Nagornykh told me that his boss the sports minister, Mutko, had phoned someone very powerful to ask for help, but how could I know if I was walking into a trap? I would have been a fool to go to the meeting alone, so I took my lawyer with me.

Mirzoyants and his entourage were waiting for us. I described our preparation for the Olympic Games, and the unique role that I played as chief of a WADA-accredited laboratory in Moscow. The London visit was essential, I explained – the chance to tour the Harlow facility was an ideal and exclusive opportunity to learn which methodology and procedures were planned in preparation for the next summer's Olympic Games, and what doping control equipment they had. Each time the IOC created a new laboratory, they prepared new traps and pitfalls for doped athletes.

We have a secret plan to improve the performance of Russian athletes, I told him, and we had to avoid the kind of doping control scandals that occurred in Athens in 2004. We have a golden opportunity to visit the laboratory in Harlow and assess any potential threats to our Russian athletes at the London Games.

I showed him my invitation from the IOC. 'Do you see my name there?' I asked. 'They're not inviting "a representative from Russia" – they're inviting *me*, as an experienced laboratory

director known to them. This is a privilege extended to me by
the IOC.'

Mirzoyants asked me whether I had my German and UK
visas.

'Yes, of course,' I replied.

He gasped long and hard, and it occurred to me that Mutko
had persuaded someone, maybe even Putin, to phone this guy.
'You may go,' he concluded reluctantly.

CHAPTER 4

STUMBLING TOWARDS SOCHI

The Cologne workshop was great: my brilliant colleague Dr Tim Sobolevsky presented a lecture on the newest long-term metabolites of anabolic steroids and received the Manfred Donike Award as the best researcher of the year in doping control, our equivalent of an Academy Award.

We went to an awards ceremony in a restaurant in a castle at the top of a hill in an ancient forest, where I drank red wine and thought about my crazy life. As soon as we'd discovered a test for the long-term metabolites, a significant analytical accomplishment, I'd started to work on a way to thwart the cutting-edge detection methods we'd discovered. This was why I was so useful to the Ministry of Sport! The 'cocktail' of three anabolic steroids with Chivas Regal was the perfect 'antidote' because it avoided the formation of long-term, traceable metabolites.

After the Manfred Donike Workshop, we WADA laboratory directors flew to London. At Cologne Bonn Airport, the officer checked my passport for five or maybe even ten minutes, which made me paranoid. I couldn't remember passport control ever taking this long – were there special notations on my passport that indicated I was still under criminal investigation? The officer flipped through the pages of my passport and tapped some information into his keyboard. I stood in front of him, breathless, feeling like that knife was plunging into my heart again. Finally, I was allowed to fly to London.

The WADA meeting in Harlow ended with a tour of the laboratory, where we could examine their instrumentation. Taking photos was prohibited, but I ignored that rule and photographed everything. We were a small group and had been instructed to stay together, because the laboratory's interior doors were locked as we proceeded from room to room. I lingered behind the rest of the group and photographed instrument after instrument, room after room.

It might sound like I was taking these pictures for espionage purposes, but I wasn't. I was just two years away from opening my own Olympic laboratory in Sochi, and had already started battling to fit it with the finest laboratory equipment available. When I returned to Moscow, I would have to start drafting purchase orders for the Ministry of Sport, to buy analytical instrumentation, laboratory equipment, furniture and chemical reagents. If questions cropped up, I would have photos of the London laboratory as proof of what we needed.

Look – the British had them. We needed them, too.

My final draft contract for Sochi included 134 separate specifications for instruments, sample preparation tools, furniture, glassware, consumables and spares, worth about $10 million. I had to buy these items in May 2012, for delivery to Sochi in November. But the laboratory was at that time nothing but a swamp – and I was still under investigation and restricted from leaving Moscow.

The FSKN inquiry hung over me like a sword of Damocles. I tried not to think about it, but I did learn that my criminal investigation had been downgraded and that my previous investigator had been replaced with one who was less severe. He seemed unfocused, and left me alone for a while, but at the end of April he decided to drag me into court again and to commit me to a four-week psychiatric observation, just as his predecessor had done. I promised him I'd return to the Serbsky Institute after the London Olympic Games and showed him my personal invitation and Olympic accreditation. He seemed surprised, but didn't back away from his plan. My problem was that I couldn't leave Moscow to attend the Games as long as I was under criminal investigation. But I had my IOC accreditation for the Olympic Games, which also functioned as a visa for the United Kingdom, and I had my plane tickets to London booked for 17 July 2012.

I decided to travel to London by any means possible, through Belarus or Ukraine if necessary. Their borders with Russia were quite permeable, and I could easily escape from Minsk or Kiev. The FSKN might arrest me when I returned to Moscow, but at that point I wouldn't care.

Then came 3 July 2012, a day I will remember forever. It was two weeks before my flight to London and I received a phone call at work. I saw the incoming phone number of my FSKN investigator and took the call in a state of suspended animation, as I always did when the FSKN called. The investigator spoke like a robot on a telemarketing call, telling me that my criminal investigation was closed and I needed to come to his office and sign the resolution papers. Then the call was over.

I couldn't believe it, and called my lawyer. He phoned the FSKN, and they confirmed it: my case was dropped and life could begin again! I left the building and filled my lungs with fresh air, drinking in the bright sun and the scuttering clouds. It was as if the world around me had changed – the trees were trembling with life and their leaves shone greener than I had ever noticed before. Nature felt warm and friendly.

I had my freedom. I was over the moon. I called Veronika and told her that I was driving over to the FSKN headquarters to pick up my resolution papers, and that we should go to a restaurant to celebrate.

'Calm down, and please drive safely,' she told me several times.

As I approached the cursed FSKN building, rage mounted within me. Then I had the papers in my hand: eight pages, double-sided, in small type. I locked the doors of my car, checked to make sure that no one was watching me and read. All my purported sins were listed in detail, followed by the determination: not enough evidence to confirm, the investigation is closed.

At home, my whole family was bouncing off the walls – it was as if I had returned from prison. Veronika, my son Vasily and my daughter Marina had been suffering and fighting alongside me. They had been summoned to interrogations, but they had invoked their right to refuse to answer questions that might bring harm to a close relative. Vasily had just graduated from Moscow University's physics department, just like his mother, and Marina had a

The criminal investigation is closed! Dazed and happy, 3 July 2012.

Moscow University chemistry degree – the same one awarded to me 29 years previously.

I made a reservation at Porto Banus, a restaurant in Krylat-skoe. It was an unforgettable family celebration. My wife and daughter were taking photos of me, while I looked completely dazed and kept hugging my dog Vrangel, who seemed to appreciate the situation better than any of us. We dangled some choice pieces of fish and meat in front of him, but he refused to eat them – it was as if he foresaw the catastrophes looming ahead of us, but was unable to warn us.

∗

With my visa and airline ticket in hand, I asked my lawyer to call and see if my name was on a 'no-fly stop' list, a pretty common trick used by the Russian security services. To be on the safe side, I took a copy of my resolution papers affirming that my criminal investigation had been dropped.

At passport control in Sheremetyevo International Airport, everything went smoothly. *Na vsaky sluchay* – 'just in case', as the Russians say – I was carrying a fifth of Balvenie 21-year-old whisky to celebrate with in London. The plane took off, and as usual, I spent the entire flight asleep. Napoleon could sleep in his carriage on the way to the battleground, and I could sleep on any flight, anywhere in the world. They laminated my accreditation at Heathrow and I headed to the Hilton overlooking Hyde Park, just a Yuriy Dumchev discus throw from Kensington Palace and the Serpentine lake. I would be staying there for three weeks, including the 14 days of the Games.

Just a few days before, I had been a phone call away from being incarcerated in a Moscow psychiatric hospital and now here I was, checking into a Hilton hotel in London as an 'IOC Family' member.

As part of the IOC Medical Commission, I received a per diem of $650 a day. When I received my $14,300 in cash, I was shocked to discover that most of the banknotes were dirty and covered with Arabic markings, random ink stamps and scribbling. This kind of suspicious cash hadn't been seen in Russia since the 1990s! So each day that I wasn't on duty at the Olympic laboratory, I went to the bank next door to the hotel and exchanged $1,500 into fresh pound notes. The teller eyed me

The Olympic Games in London, 2012. With Don Catlin, former
director of the UCLA Olympic Analytical Laboratory.

with suspicion, but my shiny IOC accreditation forced her to
smile and serve me.

The Harlow laboratory was theoretically only an hour away,
but the BMWs provided for local transportation had obsolete
navigational systems and it took the volunteer drivers two hours to
reach our destination. Once we finally got there, it was like attending a college reunion. More than 60 foreign experts from WADA
laboratories all over the world were sitting in cubicles, gossiping
and waiting for lunch. In a glass-walled room, I sat next to Professor Christiane Ayotte from Montreal. There was a special room
next door for Thierry Boghosian, the WADA independent observer who would have the same job at Sochi two years later.

Only a few foreign experts were allowed to participate in any real analytical work. The laboratory chief, Professor David Cowan, was very secretive and didn't let anyone make copies of their written procedures. Whenever we showed up inside his security perimeter, all the computer displays were switched off – he obviously didn't trust us.

Cowan seemed to avoid me but I had plenty of questions to ask him, since I would be opening the next Olympic doping control laboratory, in Sochi. One day I managed to snag him, and asked what the preliminary WADA inspections were like. He told that me that the process was simple: the inspectors had asked about security issues, camera surveillance and working conditions during the night shift.

The IOC Doping Control Group at London 2012. With Christiane Ayotte and Jordi Segura.

'That was really all they cared about,' he said.

I was taken aback. 'Are you serious? Didn't they check your proposed methodology, your protocols, your instrumentation and analytical procedures?'

Cowan smiled coolly. 'Oh, I think that would have been a bit too much for them,' he said. 'They really can't do that kind of work.'

Did this exchange make me over-confident? Perhaps.

*

When I got back to Moscow, two important tasks lay ahead. One was the construction of the new Anti-Doping Centre in Moscow and our planned move there immediately after the 2013 New Year celebration. The second task was preparing for Sochi, and the upcoming delivery of ten million dollars'-worth of instruments and laboratory equipment. The delivery was scheduled for mid-November, in 15 trucks. These items were all destined for our new building in Sochi, but where was it?

I flew to Sochi to see if the laboratory building actually existed, and how much of a threat would be posed by any delay. The builders were friendly enough and seemed hard-working, but it was clear that the laboratory wouldn't be ready by the end of November, when we needed it. I had just started taking photos of the construction site, when a security officer accosted me and told me to delete my pictures immediately. He wanted to check that there were no images left in my phone, which I promptly dropped into the pocket of my jeans.

'I'm taking photos for a report to the Olympic Committee and

My favorite picture! Terminator style. Construction of the
laboratory, September 2012.

Minister Mutko,' I told him. 'Moreover, I specially came here to
take photos of my laboratory.' He started to waver, but then
repeated that his job was specifically 'to prevent picture-taking'.

'I am the director of the Olympic laboratory,' I explained,
moving from a defensive posture to an offensive one. 'Here, where
we are standing, I am the one giving the orders – is that clear?'

He also switched tones, and explained to me in a mildly
aggrieved way that there was no laboratory planned here – this
was the proposed site of a secret building that no one was allowed
to take photos of. Only later did I learn that this would be the
FSB Command Centre, a secret police headquarters inside the

'coastal cluster' at Sochi that would share a fence with the Sochi Olympic Laboratory. Neither building existed yet: my laboratory was a skeleton and the Command Centre wasn't much more than a poured concrete foundation. Who would have believed that this half-dug hole in the ground would become ground zero for the greatest cheating scandal in Olympic history?

That was my first look at the extraordinary joint venture in Sochi, the fusion of the Ministry of Sport and the FSB and the policy of 'medals over morals'. Nobody, especially not I, could imagine how successful it would be.

CHAPTER 5

IN THE CROSSHAIRS AGAIN

Imagine my surprise when a top-level WADA inspection team showed up, unannounced, in October 2012, at 7.30 in the morning darkness at the gates of the Moscow Anti-Doping Centre. Emerging like unwanted ghosts from underneath the shadows of the trees were WADA's scientific director Dr Olivier Rabin, Thierry Boghosian, the manager for Laboratory Accreditation, and Victoria Ivanova, the manager for Scientific Projects.

Rabin whipped out a list of 67 urine samples of Russian athletes collected before the London Olympics, and asked for the leftover ones, which WADA had instructed us to retain, to be shipped to Lausanne for reanalysis. He and his colleagues obviously suspected the Russians of being dirty, and they intended to prove it. They also realised that the Olympic doping control in Harlow had been inadequate.

The DHL office in Moscow informed us that they couldn't pick up urine samples immediately, so we arranged to have them picked up the next day. That gave us less than 24 hours to make the urine look doping-free; it was one of the most challenging nights of my life.

Rabin wanted the samples belonging to track and field athletes, but I knew there were between 10 and 12 positives among them, which we had misreported as negatives before the London Games. The national team coach Alexey Melnikov had spent the summer collecting clean samples from these athletes, anticipating our fears that their urine might be requisitioned for reanalysis.

We had plenty of plastic bottles full of 'clean' urine that we could pour into the A bottles, taking care to fill them to the level left over after testing procedures. The 'clean' urine collected before the London Games was doping-free, with the exception of the sample belonging to Darya Pishchalnikova, a discus thrower whose clean urine contained traces of oxandrolone. Our biggest challenge was to make the tampered A bottled urine look like the B samples, because they had been collected at different times, in some cases months apart.

We couldn't open the B bottles, so had to make the A and B samples look similar enough to get past the trained eyes of the laboratory professionals in Lausanne. Just a glance could tell you that the samples were different – the colours didn't match, and the tiny suspended flakes that formed after storage were different shapes and sizes, just as no two snowflakes are alike if you take a closer look. I spent all night conducting experiments, for instance tweaking pH readings, which helped change the appearance of the flakes. Then I tried to make the samples paler or darker, either by diluting them with water or adding Nescafé instant coffee granules to the bottles. Then I drove back home to catch two hours of sleep, under Vrangel's watchful eye.

The next day Rabin had a chatty, 'we're-all-friends-here' meeting with Vitaly Mutko, before supervising the samples' transfer to DHL. Rabin seemed relaxed and satisfied, but I was paralysed by anxiety. Who had turned us in, and what explained the surprise? This kind of visit had never happened to any WADA-accredited laboratory, and we certainly didn't want it happening to us again in the future.

There was ample evidence that WADA had us in their crosshairs. In the meantime, the laboratory in Lausanne completed its reanalysis of the 55 samples that had enough urine left in A bottles and, as predicted, came up with one firm positive: Pishchalnikova, the discus silver medallist in London. The laboratory detected tiny amounts of oxandrolone metabolites in her swapped A sample bottle. Mutko was furious, but I wrote a standard WADA-format letter, explaining that I had reported her negative based on a Minimum Required Performance Limit (MRPL) threshold from 2010. They were not convinced.

Pishchalnikova and her lawyer, Alexander Chebotarev, travelled to Lausanne to witness the B analysis. She went ballistic when her supposedly 'clean' sample also tested positive. It was no surprise; her body was basically a steroid-soaked sponge. She wrote a letter to WADA and the IAAF, explaining that she had been coerced by Melnikov into participating in the Russian doping programme, and that I had agreed to cover up her positive results. Furthermore, she accused me of threatening to falsify her steroid profile unless she paid me off. This was lunacy – I had never come within 50 feet of her in my life, and hadn't even spoken to her on the phone.

The volatile Mutko flew into another rage and gave me a dressing down. He was a simple fellow, a Putin loyalist who had backed me in my battle against the FSKN. I told him that Pishchalnikova was lying through her teeth about any commitments I made to her. I also explained to him, as I had told Melnikov, that she had been playing with fire because her 'clean' urine didn't match her urine steroid profile previously uploaded to the ADAMS database. She was a chronic doper, who was bound to be caught eventually.

Mutko devised an acceptable solution: Pishchalnikova would get to keep the rewards of her tainted career: her cars, apartments and Olympic bonus payments. (Her mother, whom Pishchalnikova listed as her coach, reaped a similar bounty from the state.) In return, she would write a second letter to WADA and the IAAF, disavowing her earlier charges. She told them that someone had hacked into her email account and transmitted those crazy accusations.

*

The larger problem remained: if WADA had us in their crosshairs, all my plans for our Sochi laboratory would be derailed.

I generally reported to Mutko through the deputy minister Yuri Nagornykh, so the day after the WADA staff left, I went to his office to emphasise how much trouble we were in. If someone noticed the visual discrepancies between the urine specimens in the A and B bottles we sent in, WADA would almost certainly suspend or revoke its accreditation of the Moscow Anti-Doping Centre and terminate the preparations for our Sochi Olympics laboratory. That would mean that all Russian athletes' doping control samples would be analysed in Austrian or German laboratories, with unpredictable results. The catastrophe would hit our track and field and weightlifting teams first, and spread from there.

Even if we survived this crisis, I explained, the technology of the tamper-proof BEREG-kit bottles would trip us up sooner or later. Now we could only substitute clean urine in A bottles and report false negatives from the A samples in our possession, while the B bottles remained ticking time bombs. To really beat the system, I explained, we would need to open the plastic cap, swap the urine and reseal the B bottles, so having the same clean urine in A and B bottles. If this was possible – and I was sure that it was not – it would mean the end of doping control forever.

WADA had left, but I continued to worry. I felt like an insect pinned under a microscope, and didn't know who was examining us. But Nagornykh told me, cryptically, that our problems would be solved and his words had a soothing effect, the way a sympathetic father might assure you that he had anticipated all your problems and was doing his best to resolve them.

Just keep doing what you are doing, Nagornykh said. Relax and enjoy your trip to Zurich to visit the ski federation people. I did enjoy the trip, and it later became clear: Nagornykh knew plenty that I didn't.

PART III

CONJURER

CHAPTER 1

OPERATION SOCHI RESULTAT

In 2013, the countdown to the Sochi Games had begun. We spent the Orthodox Christmas holiday moving our instruments into the new four-storey Moscow ADC, constructed behind the VNIIFK building, where the laboratory had been housed since 1979. I informed WADA that we had relocated, and they planned an inspection for late January. In anticipation, Blokhin, the FSB officer assigned to monitor my laboratory and RUSADA, installed eavesdropping equipment in the rooms where the WADA inspectors would be interviewing my personnel.

After visiting both new laboratory buildings in Sochi and Moscow, the WADA team left. A few days later, Blokhin came to my office, beaming.

'Why are you so happy – was your wiretapping successful?' I asked him.

'Relax – maybe I'll tell you later.' He scampered off to the gym, but accepted my invitation to lunch at a local Azeri restaurant, famous for its tequila, green salad and succulent lamb.

On that winter's day in Moscow, roughly a year before the start of the Sochi Games, the world of sport changed forever. I plied Blokhin with tequila, hoping to learn about WADA's plans, but he refused to talk about the wiretapping. Blokhin was laconic. He didn't engage in small talk, and he generally didn't ask questions. (Ask not, lest ye be asked . . .) However, after cautiously surveying the restaurant, he edged his chair closer to mine and told me that his team of 'magicians' had managed to successfully open BEREG-kit B sample bottles.

I was flabbergasted. This breakthrough was like the splitting of the atom. If true, it would change the arc of my life and the future of Russian sport.

I decided to test him. 'I have two filthy samples back in the laboratory,' I said, 'from two track and field athletes whom we reported negative. But their urine is full of dope – can you unscrew caps from their B bottles for me?'

Blokhin did not answer and just stared at me, as if he hadn't heard the question.

'Please, open these bottles for me. I even have the athletes' clean urine ready for swapping.'

He remained silent, as if he regretted spilling the beans in the first place. After a pause, I tried a different tack. 'Does Deputy Minister Nagornykh know about your success?'

Still Blokhin stayed quiet.

'Look, if you can't take these two B bottles, I could approach Nagornykh and he could officially request that they be opened?'

My taciturn companion suddenly spoke. 'No one else needs to

get involved. I'll take your damned bottles, but for now, this stays between us.'

I escorted him back to the ADC, handed over the bottles in a double plastic bag and thanked him, before following him out our front door – I wanted to be sure that he didn't change his mind.

Nagornykh's intimation that our B bottle problems might soon be solved had hinted at this breakthrough. My associates had told me that Blokhin had been collecting the metal rings with teeth and the lock springs from discarded BEREG-kit A plastic caps, in addition to closed B bottles from out-of-date storage samples that were awaiting disposal. My friend Dr Nikita Kamaev, the executive director of RUSADA, also told me that Blokhin was collecting new BEREG-kit bottles of various designs.

However, figuring out how to open them with no trace of damage had until now remained an apparently impossible task. I knew that Berlinger, the Zurich-based manufacturer of the BEREG-kit bottles, had always insisted that the technology they used meant that no one could tamper with their sample bottles and avoid detection. Despite a mountain of evidence to the contrary, they make that claim to this day.

A few days later, Blokhin returned with the bottles. FSB engineers had opened both of them cleanly, and Blokhin, his face alight with a conspiratorial smile, handed me the undamaged caps. I was shocked as I carefully inspected the surface of the glass bottle and its plastic cap inside – they were separated, but they appeared to be intact. Blokhin told me that the removal had proceeded smoothly, after which they had erased any visible scratches. They

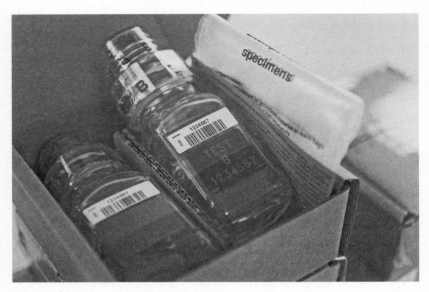

The 'tamper-proof' BEREG-kit bottles, with their lock springs and
metal rings with teeth.

had damaged the serrated metal ring inside the plastic cap but
had substituted a replacement one, shiny and intact.

Blokhin left my office, and I ran to the Ministry of Sport to
inform Nagornykh. This was the same path I had taken on
30 October 1985, when I went to apply for the job of junior
researcher at the VNIIFK doping control laboratory. Nagornykh
now occupied the office formerly assigned to the VNIIFK director; he was ecstatic at the news and congratulated us profusely
before sprinting down the hallway to report to Mutko, who I'm
sure passed the word to President Putin.

Three years later, the filmmaker Bryan Fogel asked chief
investigator Richard McLaren, appointed by WADA, what would
happen if doping laboratories could switch out B samples at will.

McLaren replied that it would render all doping control 'illusory'. Truer words had never been spoken.

*

This was the key that slipped the lock for Operation Sochi Resultat.

A Sochi Games triumvirate was forming: me, Nagornykh and Irina Rodionova, a former champion swimmer, doctor and close associate of Nagornykh's who had been brought in as our liaison with the winter sports teams. We had to focus on the opportunity offered by Sochi: between 30 January and late February of 2014, all the Olympic doping control samples would be passing through our laboratory. And from the week before the Games until a few days after they closed, WADA would have no jurisdiction in Sochi – we'd have to file our analyses with ADAMS, but would report results to the IOC and to no one else. We needed to exploit this situation, on behalf of Russian athletes.

By early 2013, we knew that we had a nearly undetectable steroid delivery system in the 'cocktail', as well as backup protection if we needed it; we could remove and swap tainted urine from an athlete's A and B bottles. Irina performed some mental calculations before announcing matter-of-factly that Russia would win 15 gold medals in Sochi. I was shocked – we had won just three gold medals at the previous Winter Olympic Games in Vancouver in 2010 – but she was confident, and she would turn out to be pretty much right.

Despite our confidence, the three of us agreed that the Russian doping programme was clearly under siege, as the surprise

WADA visit to the Moscow Centre had shown. Someone, in all likelihood an insider, was reporting on us. We formulated an action plan to carry us through the Sochi Games:

1. When necessary, we would falsify an athlete's dirty urine in both the A and B bottles. One method would be substitution – the athlete pours in clean urine from a freezer and seals the bottles at the collection sites. This could be done in the presence of a corrupt RUSADA doping control officer and would make my life easier, since there would be no need to misreport a negative result to ADAMS followed by the headache of the ticking time bomb of a sealed B bottle – because it would contain 'clean' urine. As a last line of defence, if dirty urine from a protected athlete was delivered to the Moscow laboratory, we could misreport and swap the samples with 'clean' urine from CSP freezers, but that would require the assistance of FSB experts in opening the sealed B bottles.

2. No WADA-appointed DCOs or IDTM or Munich-based PWC agents would be allowed to remove doping control samples from Russian soil, under any circumstances.

3. We would use the 'Duchess' cocktail for the steroid programme. It was easily administered, and washed out of the athlete's body within a few days.

All systems were go.

*

While our battle with WADA simmered in the background, our plans for the Sochi Games became more and more brazen. On 4 April, Nagornykh called me into his office and unveiled his latest idea. There happened to be a big biathlon event in Moscow, and the biathlon – cross-country skiing combined with marksmanship – was a huge fan favourite in Russia; but sadly for Russia's medal; hopes at Sochi, two of the world's promising biathletes, the twin sisters Valya and Vita Semerenko, were Ukrainian.

Nagornykh knew that my laboratory could turn a positive sample into a negative, and because he was focused on winning at all costs, the opposite idea had occurred to him.

'At the Anti-Doping Centre,' he asked carefully, 'could we make the Semerenkos' clean results dirty?'

I was shocked and frightened – I didn't know where this would lead. 'For what purpose?'

Nagornykh explained. 'These Ukrainian biathletes are going to be ferocious competitors at Sochi, and Vita Semerenko is in Moscow right now. I could ask RUSADA to take her sample and then let you know her code number . . .'

He gazed at me, awaiting my response. It was the only time in my life when I regretted not having a pocket tape recorder. What Nagornykh was suggesting was illegal and unethical – and in the bare-knuckle world of Russian sport, it was a very dangerous suggestion. If the Ukrainians ever traced the false positives back to me, they would set fire to my car – or much worse.

I needed the world to know that this was Nagornykh's idea, and that I opposed it. Yes, I had turned hundreds of positive samples into negative ones, but I never did the opposite, or even had any thought of such a thing. None of my friends or colleagues had ever asked me to make the urine samples of innocent athletes look like they were doping either! In my mind, I unreeled the riot act that I should have read to Nagornykh.

I tried to explain to Nagornykh why this was a bad idea, but chose my words carefully – no one wants an enemy with the title 'Deputy Minister'.

'It would be hard to disguise the fact that her urine sample hadn't passed through her body, but had been spiked from the outside. Furthermore, as top-tier athletes, the sisters are in the International Testing Registered Pool. Suppose they were targeted for an out-of-competition test a few days after our Moscow laboratory accused them of doping and tested clean, with no traces of the substances we claimed to have discovered in their urine?'

Nagornykh retained his poker face.

'That would trigger an immediate investigation of us,' I said. 'It would present a grave danger, both for our Sochi plans and for everything that lies ahead. I can't see making that work right now, so let's stay focused on Sochi and not make trouble for ourselves.'

I held my breath. Thank God, Nagornykh finally relaxed and agreed with me.

To be fair, his high opinion of the Ukrainian biathletes proved correct. Their women won the biathlon relay in Sochi – four gold medals for four girls!

I left Nagornykh's office and took a deep breath. Occasionally, when under stress, my childhood asthma re-asserted itself; only when I filled my lungs with outdoor air could I marshal my thoughts. Yes, of course I could make clean urine look dirty, but it was an outlandish request and the risks far outweighed the possible rewards. I needed to talk to someone, so I approached my laboratory colleague Dr Tim Sobolevsky and asked him a 'theoretical' question about how he might go about deliberately tainting urine samples. He found the question odd, and asked where it came from.

'Guess,' I said.

'Nagornykh,' he replied. 'It couldn't be anyone else.'

I described the 'Ukrainian proposal' to my childhood friend, the RUSADA director Nikita Kamaev, who had had his eye on our esteemed deputy minister since he attended a special sports school as a high jumper.

'Nagornykh understands nothing,' Nikita told me. 'You could doctor the urine in an A bottle, but the B bottle would still contain clean urine!' Nikita did not know that we had just figured out how to open the impregnable B bottles.

'Do you know why Nagornykh got kicked out of sports school?' Nikita asked me. 'He was caught stealing running shoes from his teammate. Then he went on to flourish in the Komsomol [the Young Communists League], a typical career for an ambitious sports apparatchik.'

*

WADA kept on coming to see us – someone was whispering in their ear. In that same month, they sent a bulked-up inspection team to Moscow, this time adding John Miller, the head of WADA's Laboratory Expert Group, and Professor Jordi Segura, director of the Olympic doping control laboratory in

Barcelona, to their team. This was their third on-site inspection in six months, which seemed suspicious. After all, the Moscow Anti-Doping Centre was the most productive anti-doping laboratory in the world – in 2011 and 2012, we had analysed 15,370 and 17,175 urine samples, more than any other WADA-accredited laboratory.

Fulfilling quotas was one thing, but we couldn't shake our reputation for questionable analyses. For example: From the batch of 67 samples WADA had seized the previous year, they analysed 55 and found oxandrolone metabolite in Pishchalnikova's sample, but they weren't able to analyse the remaining 12 samples because there wasn't enough urine left in the A bottle. Rabin then ordered the 12 B bottles to be split into B1 and B2 for analysis, revealing two more positives that we had misreported.

Rabin smelled blood. After he found these two misreported positives, he ordered the Lausanne laboratory to reanalyse the previous 54 samples (not including Pishchalnikova's) in the same way, by splitting the B bottles. We, Moscow and Lausanne, had reported all 54 samples to be negative, but if the B bottles were reanalysed, then Lausanne laboratory would find eight to ten positives. That in itself would be a catastrophe, but when they realised that the A and B samples contained *different urine* – that we had falsified the samples *after* being asked to preserve them – WADA would close down the Moscow ADC in a heartbeat and our planning to obtain accreditation for the Sochi laboratory would be over.

But then a miracle occurred. In conformance with WADA rules, the Lausanne laboratory had destroyed our 54 'negative' samples after storing them for three months. WADA had been informed that if they wanted to retain the samples they would have to pay for extended storage, but they never responded and our problems were tossed into the garbage.

One problem had been solved, but another took its place when WADA put our EPO detection methodology under the microscope. We happened to be doing some routine testing while they were in our laboratory, and – *voilà*! – a textbook positive result appeared. The sample belonged to a female biathlete who had been tested in-competition, and we were happy that WADA had witnessed the analysis, by way of proving our expertise and honesty. Our visitors assumed that we would download the results to ADAMS, after seeking the mandatory second opinion from a WADA expert in Barcelona, but would we?

The positive belonged to our 'biathlon princess' Svetlana Sleptsova, but there was no way we could report her positive because she was under the direct protection of Mutko. As I have already explained, biathlon was a sacred cow in Russia – not only did Sleptsova command a huge TV audience, but the powerful oligarch Mikhail Prokhorov was president of the Russian Biathlon Union. We were in a real bind. The WADA team had witnessed this positive analysis with their own eyes, and they wouldn't forget it. Sleptsova was untouchable, but with the Sochi Games less than a year away, we couldn't afford a doping scandal.

I explained the situation to Kamaev and asked him whether RUSADA could falsify Sleptsova's doping control form (DCF), by inserting a different name and a non-winter sport. We couldn't make the positive disappear, but we could assign it to someone else, maybe someone in a non-Olympic sport.

'We might have got away with that a year ago,' Nikita explained, 'when the laboratory sent the positive results to ADAMS, and RUSADA could take a while before sharing the athletes' names with the international authorities.' But that was no longer the way things worked. 'WADA now insists the national anti-doping agencies download all documents, and names especially, to ADAMS immediately, even before delivering the samples for analysis to the laboratory.'

'So, *Grinya*, no way to help you, my friend, sorry for that,' he concluded.

I was called *Grinya* in our apartment building's courtyard 40 years ago.

But don't forget: This was Russia, the land of miracles.

I explained the problem to Nagornykh, who put the squeeze on RUSADA until they reluctantly falsified the case documentation in September. After their creative rewrite, Sleptsova's positive disappeared and was replaced by a thirty-something female sambo wrestler suspected of EPO use. Of course, we had to explain our misreporting and delay in a corrective action report (CAR), which was one of the most challenging documents I have ever written. It took me ten drafts to describe our web of obfuscations, which George Orwell had captured so well in *1984*, when he talked about being able 'to forget whatever it was necessary to forget, then to draw it back into memory again at the moment when it was needed, and then promptly to forget it again.'

That was my CAR#19 in a nutshell.

CHAPTER 2

THE TWO-FRONT WAR

The war with WADA would continue almost until the opening ceremony in Sochi. But wars are fought on many fronts, and a spectacular bomb exploded in July, when we least expected it. The integrity of the upcoming Sochi Games, the British *Daily Mail* reported, had 'been plunged into doubt by allegations that Russian athletes are doping under instruction from coaches and are assisted by cover-ups at the country's main anti-doping laboratory.'

The exposé had two main thrusts: First, it quoted several Russian athletes who said that they had been forced to participate in a national doping programme. Oleg Popov was quoted as saying, 'Not only does an athlete have to take illegal drugs, he also has to pay money in our anti-doping laboratory for substituting the samples.' This accusation was made by the coach of Lada Chernova, the javelin thrower who tried to destroy her tainted sample in my laboratory twice, indoors and outdoors, while I watched.

The *Mail*'s second line of attack was aimed directly at me. 'The boss of the key [doping control] laboratory,' the newspaper reported, 'was arrested and questioned on suspicion of sourcing and selling banned drugs,' referring to my 2011 confrontations with the FSKN. The article highlighted my suicide attempt, my institutionalisation and my sister Marina's arrest for 'buying and possessing banned drugs that she admitted she had intended to supply to athletes.'

The *Mail* fretted that honest British athletes, such as runner Lynsey Sharp or long jumper Gregory Rutherford, would lose medals to drugged-up Russian competitors. The *Mail* asked out loud if notorious dopers like the Russians could be trusted to operate an Olympic laboratory at the Sochi Winter Games. They then quoted an IOC spokesman, who predicted there would be no problems:

> 'There will be at least 20 international experts working in labs throughout the time of the Games to ensure the very best methods and practices . . . In addition, there will be three experts in the IOC Games Group whose specific task will be to oversee and guarantee the integrity of all processes of analyses and reporting to the IOC.'

This was true, but to catch our cheating would take someone as deeply steeped in it as we were! WADA would never have any real oversight in my laboratory. Just as Professor David Cowan kept people like me and Professor Christiane Ayotte at arm's length from his analyses in the Harlow laboratory, I was careful who I invited to Sochi. I didn't want anyone sniffing under the table or peeking behind doors.

The article itself was less important than its timing and where it appeared. This wasn't journalism – this was a sucker punch in a mixed-martial arts cage match. I was reasonably sure that the 'facts' had been leaked by my old adversary Alexander Chebotarev, a clever lawyer who was waging a running battle against RUSADA, representing such athletes as Lada Chernova and Darya Pishchalnikova. I never regarded him as an enemy, and he taught me a lot, but – he just seemed eager to earn money, become famous and occupy a very profitable niche in the world of sports jurisprudence.

With the Olympic Games just seven months away, someone claimed they had informed WADA of irregularities in the Russian doping programme, and that WADA had turned a deaf ear. Well, not any more. The *Daily Mail* website had millions of readers all over the world; the door on the 'Russian doping scandal' had cracked open.

It closed again, quickly. There would be no follow-up to the *Mail*'s story, but someone was definitely out to get us. First we had been subjected to the surprise inspection and the ongoing WADA investigation, and then we had been publicly accused of cheating. Life was about to get even more interesting – and not in a good way.

*

In September 2013, WADA conducted a fourth pre-Olympic inspection of our laboratory. The visitors were Thierry Boghosian and John Miller from WADA and Professor Jordi Segura from Barcelona, who was also the president of the World

Association of Anti-Doping Scientists (WAADS). They presented us with a list of 56 alleged discrepancies in laboratory operation routine, 33 of which we had resolved acceptably with corrective action reports. In their view, 15 discrepancies remained unaddressed, and eight others had only been partially fixed. They were particularly irate about the misreporting of Sleptsova's EPO case, and they were far from convinced by our 'discovery' that the positive result belonged to an unknown sambo wrestler.

They were threatening to suspend the accreditation of the Moscow Anti-Doping Centre, which would automatically shut down our brand-new, $30 million laboratory in Sochi.

Segura told me straight out that WADA was preparing an attack on the Moscow laboratory. Our fate would be decided at WADA's fourth World Conference on Doping in Sport in Johannesburg, scheduled for mid-November. There had never been a showdown of this magnitude in the brief history of sport doping control. I would be facing a Disciplinary Committee consisting of former WADA president Dick Pound, the British barrister Jonathan Taylor and the USADA scientist Dr Larry Bowers.

I figured Bowers, who understood bench chemistry and whom I had known since the 1990s, would support me, but I couldn't take any chances with the seasoned international lawyers Pound and Taylor and retained my lawyer, Claude Ramoni. Testifying against us was the Laboratory Experts Group, consisting of Olivier Rabin and John Miller. They clearly declared their intentions – they wanted a six-month suspension of our accreditation. This was just like facing the accursed Basmanny

District Court in Moscow, where the sentence had been decided beforehand.

I was angry. It was true that, as lawyers say, I came to these proceedings with 'unclean hands', but I felt our sins were few and our accomplishments many. We were about to open the best Olympic laboratory ever built. The FSKN had nearly driven me to suicide; this WADA onslaught felt like more of the same.

Learning that my fate had already been baked into their deliberations, I launched my counterattack: my *Summa Contra WADA*, named after the famous arguments of ancient philosophers against false scientific concepts. I had plenty of help from three professors, Christiane Ayotte, Jordi Segura and Martial Saugy from Lausanne, and we proved to be a far stronger team than the LabEx functionaries.

My main points were:

1. The Moscow ADC was one of the most innovative and productive laboratories in the world. I challenged WADA's concept of the 'negative' analytical result, pointing out that there was no definition of such a result in WADA's International Standard for Laboratories. As anti-doping detection technology becomes ever more sensitive and precise, any negative can in theory become positive after reanalysis.

2. Almost all the 'errors' attributed to us could be explained by discrepancies in the sensitivity of our instruments. The technology in the Sochi laboratory would be better; the latest models were purchased. But our Moscow ADC equipment was a mixture of old and new tools, since we were using the

newest instrumentation for research and development of methods. At the time when WADA launched its crusade against us, we used old models for everyday analyses and we were overwhelmed by the move into a new building.

3. I emphasised that WADA's accusation of 'false negative results' in the Sleptsova EPO sample was 'unacceptable', and fully resolved and explained in my corrective action report.

I think the transcripts of those hearings may one day be included in textbooks. It cost me a lot of money, aggravation and time that should have been spent preparing the Sochi laboratory; all I could think about was that if I failed, the Moscow Anti-Doping Centre would be ruined, my 50 employees would lose their jobs and my high-wire act of balancing the competing interests of doping control and the medal-obsessed Russian sport bureaucracy would come to a crashing halt. As they say in Hollywood, I would never work in this town again.

I flew to Johannesburg two days early to meet Claude Ramoni and we discussed the issues and decided what we would say during the hearings. Despite my misgivings, the Independent Disciplinary Committee turned out to seem quite impartial. The chairman, Dick Pound, didn't talk much and appeared to zone out during the discussions. Larry Bowers was the only member who had worked in a doping control laboratory; he sat close to me and seemed independent, reluctantly supporting me or explaining the technical points I was making. The other commissioner, Jonathan Taylor, acted like a referee, monitoring the timing of the presentations and trying to soothe tempers when arguments became emotional or unproductive.

Olivier Rabin often ignored the documents that were under discussion, and instead invoked mysterious intelligence data about cover-ups in the Moscow laboratory. As we would later learn, some low-level whistle-blowers had indeed been feeding him information. He assumed a serious political face when referring to these shadowy charges, but it didn't seem to have much effect on this audience. The agenda items had been pre-approved and Rabin's wool-gathering didn't seem welcome.

I remember feeling sick to death of WADA's hypocritical pettiness regarding doping control. They spent all their time feigning concern about the 1 per cent of positive analyses they received from laboratories, when they knew full well that between 30 and 40 per cent of athletes were doping in sports like track and field. One of their key accusations against us consisted of six positive results, following the reanalysis of 2,959 samples using triple-quadrupole mass spectrometer analyses, which only two laboratories in the world could have performed – ours and Cologne. Furthermore, those six positives surfaced only thanks to our own analysis of the long-term metabolites of steroids! We had actually discovered 20 positives, but Nagornykh only allowed us to report six of them.

In the end, the Disciplinary Committee formally suspended the Moscow laboratory for six months, but then postponed their own suspension for six months, to give us time to engage 'independent quality management' experts to address our alleged shortcomings. This was a good result – I had six months of breathing space that extended beyond the Olympic and Paralympic Games in Sochi, which was all I needed.

As I rejoiced in my diary, 'Now I am playing with white pieces!' Yes, I am Russian to the core – I love eating borscht and playing chess.

The indecision was symptomatic of WADA at its worst. I had been censured but could keep working. They brayed about 'clean' sport, but lacked the will to act. I didn't want to protest too much, of course. On to Sochi!

*

Blokhin and his magicians at the FSB were perfecting the dark art of opening the B bottles. The illicit uncapping was slow at first, requiring one or two hours to open just a couple of bottles. Even worse, the magicians showed their hands sometimes, leaving scratches or cracking the plastic cap. However, their performance and speed soon dramatically improved.

Blokhin had used the summer Universiade Games, which had been held in Kazan in July, to gain expertise in sample collection at an international multisport event. We concluded that the substitution of dirty urine for a clean specimen at Sochi's remote collection stations, where there would be 16 doping control stations in all, could blow up in our faces, so we decided to swap the samples inside our Sochi laboratory, where we could control any threats and uncertainties.

It was time to figure out the logistics and to 'think outside the box', as Dr Olivier Rabin was so fond of saying.

My staff and I spent the months preceding the Games

Our four-storey, state-of-the-art laboratory in Sochi.

shuttling between Sochi and Moscow. Our Sochi laboratory was actually 20 miles from the centre of Sochi in the suburb of Adler, where Sochi International Airport and the 'coastal cluster' of Olympic venues were located. The wonderful Adelphia Hotel, just 300 feet from the Black Sea, became my second home.

My long-time assistant, the former world-class marathon runner Yuri Chizhov, drilled the famous 'mousehole' in the wall, about eight inches off the ground. The hole connected the strictly controlled Room 125 inside the security perimeter, where samples were 'aliquoted' or apportioned, and our 'operational' Room 124, which was not surveilled by security cameras. Samples that needed to be swapped could move from the tightly monitored aliquoting area to the neighbouring room, and then Blokhin could remove them to the FSB's Command Centre in the next door building, where we kept four freezers full of clean, pre-tested urine and where the magicians could work through the night.

[Left] Yury Chizhov, who drilled the mousehole, in 2013.
[Right] Evgeny Blokhin in my office, Moscow 2013.

Blokhin, masquerading as a plumber, would spend the nights in the laboratory, assuring the smooth transfer of BEREG-kit bottles to the Command Centre and back again. On 30 December I gave Deputy Minister Yuri Nagornykh a briefing on our preparations. He gave us his blessing and gathered the lab's key personnel for a photo. It was funny to see Chizhov wearing a suit and tie, but a visit from a deputy minister required a certain protocol!

On Christmas Eve, we conducted a night-time 'stress test' in the Sochi laboratory, simulating the precise conditions of the

Olympic Games. At midnight, we accepted and registered 96 urine and 44 blood samples, opened them, aliquoted them and sent them upstairs for analysis via a special elevator. My hard-working team of young girls and boys were enjoying fulfilling their life's dream of working at the Olympic Games!

But while I watched the rehearsal, I was estimating how many BEREG-kit bottles with dirty urine could be surreptitiously removed from the reception area, and for how long? How much time would we need to move those bottles to the Command Centre to be clandestinely opened and bring them back for swapping and resealing? I estimated we would have two hours each night – any more would be dangerous – which meant we could swap 10 to 12 urine samples a night, and no more. All samples had to be aliquoted and transferred for instrumental analysis by 7am at the latest.

This operation would be as delicately choreographed as the most intricate performance at the Bolshoi Ballet, but instead of dancers, we were using the secret police.

CHAPTER 3

LET THE GAMES BEGIN

It is impossible to overstate what the Sochi Winter Olympic Games meant to Russians and to the regime of Vladimir Putin. Russia had edged out Salzburg in Austria and Pyeongchang in South Korea for selection in 2007, the final year of Putin's second term as president. Although it was not obvious at the time, 2007 was the beginning of the Putin era, with all that now implies. Buoyed by nationalist sentiment, rising oil prices and a keen sense for how much dictatorship the Russian people could stomach, Putin was on the verge of becoming president for life, and the Games were a glittering jewel in his crown.

Just as importantly, the Sochi Olympics would be the first Games to be held on Russian soil since the collapse of the Soviet Union in 1991. Russian memories were long enough to recall the embarrassment of the Western boycott of the Moscow Games in 1980, following the Soviet invasion of Afghanistan. The Sochi Games in 2014 would be different; Russia was a bona fide member of the world community, and every nation with a winter sports team planned to compete.

It is also important to recall the Russian failure at the 2010

Winter Olympic Games in Vancouver, where our athletes won
three gold out of 15 medals in total and failed to finish among the
top ten countries on the medal table. After the then president,
Dmitri Medvedev, blamed a slew of top-level bureaucrats, who
quickly retired, it became obvious that Putin had much higher
expectations for Sochi. It was no coincidence that on the day he
was inaugurated in 2012, his first visitor was the IOC president,
Jacques Rogge.

Holding the Games in Sochi was an extraordinary act of
hubris, demonstrating the boundless self-confidence of Putin's
one-man rule. Sochi was a summer resort on the Black Sea with a
latitude similar to the French Riviera that had since Stalin's era
earned a reputation as a beach resort for Soviet workers and Communist Party bosses. There were mountains nearby, but they were
covered with wild forest. The chutzpah of staging a Winter Olympic Games at Sochi was like hosting the Iditarod dog-sledding
championships in Miami Beach, and yet it happened.

It seemed fitting that just before I left for Sochi, we had to
confront yet another embarrassing doping scandal. As part of our
settlement with WADA, two foreign anti-doping experts came
to the Moscow ADC in early January to conduct an inspection,
presenting us with an opportunity to show how we handled samples, from reception to reporting the results.

Predictably, disaster struck, when we found the new doping
compound GW1516 in a female sample. I called Nagornykh and
told him we had demonstrated a positive result in the presence of
foreign inspectors and would have to download it to the ADAMS
database.

Unsurprisingly, the tainted specimen belonged to one of coach Viktor Chegin's many Saransk race walkers, the reigning Olympic champion and world record holder Elena Lashmanova. The next day I was asked to make the result disappear. I had saved her by misreporting her positive findings twice before, but that wouldn't be possible this time, as foreign experts had witnessed the analysis.

The explanation for how this had happened astounded me – it transpired that Chegin himself had substituted the urine sample. Lashmanova had treated an injury with the corticosteroid Dexamethasone, which Chegin didn't realise athletes were allowed to use in out-of-competition periods. To salvage the situation, he substituted one of Lashmanova's allegedly 'clean specimens' taken after the London Olympic Games, which he kept in a freezer for such occasions, unaware that Lashmanova had been using GW1516 before London, which the Olympic laboratory in Harlow had not been able to detect.

In retrospect, the London Games turned to be the dirtiest in history: reanalysis showed that 126 positives[3] were misreported as negatives due to the Harlow laboratory's poor analytical performance in 2012. With 82 positives, the largest proportion belonged to track and field.

But Chegin believed the London results and thought the urine was clean, a clear case of misplaced confidence in his 'unique and outstanding' methodology and his commitment to

3 https://www.insidethegames.biz/articles/1090223/athletics-2012-doping-ban (accessed 7 Feb 2020).

bespredel', i.e. doping 'at any cost'. It also showed how little he knew about the basic doping control rules previously set by WADA.

A couple of days after the inspectors left, Nagornykh, Rodionova and I met at the Ministry of Sport to seal Lashmanova's fate. There was no way we could save her – WADA was putting out too much heat. We had narrowly escaped catastrophe in Johannesburg just two months earlier; one more suspicious case would probably cost the Moscow Anti-Doping Centre its accreditation, and would end my career.

I said goodbye and left for the airport, where Dr Rabin was waiting for me. We flew to Sochi, to perform the final accreditation trial.

*

The Games would start on 7 February, but pre-competition analyses were scheduled from 31 January, when the Olympic Village would start to fill up with athletes. Receiving the final accreditation from Rabin would be a milestone for our four-storey, state-of-the art laboratory. We analysed the test samples without a hitch and then the entire staff assembled for a photo to commemorate the occasion.

That night, after we had received our Certificate of Accreditation, Rabin and I stayed up late in the bar of the Radisson Hotel and drank two bottles of red wine. We discussed everything, from his attempt to indict me in Johannesburg to how to keep WADA happy during the Games. Then, a few glasses later and completely out of the blue, he inquired whether the

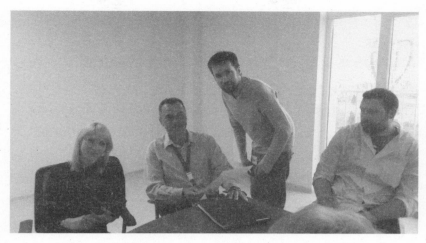

Dr Tim Sobolevsky reporting our results. The next minute,
Dr Olivier Rabin signed the Certificate of Accreditation.
Sochi, January 2014.

Moscow laboratory had ever tried to report positive results as negative.

What could I say? That I had falsified hundreds of positive results during my tenure as director of the Moscow Laboratory? That Russian sports bureaucrats had dreamed up an ambitious and fraudulent 'Sochi Resultat' plan for the forthcoming Olympics, involving an FSB taskforce and magicians employed to open sealed bottles? Choosing my words carefully, I explained that life is not easy and nobody is perfect – Russia is Russia. I said that I couldn't give him any details, but reluctantly admitted that I was 'part of the system'.[4]

Then I shuttled back to Moscow to deliver the updated 'Sochi 2014 version' of the new BEREG-kits to Blokhin, so his magicians could get in some final pre-Olympic training – just like the athletes! He and I reviewed every detail of our forthcoming adventure. We agreed that the 'bank' of clean urine specimens for swapping would arrive in Sochi at the end of January, and would be kept in the adjacent FSB headquarters, the so-called 'Command Centre'. We had installed a new security system to monitor the fridges and freezers inside the Olympic laboratory. It gave us real-time readings of the temperatures inside the coolers, and

---

4 This brief moment of candour proved to be ill-advised. Almost two years later, my after-hours chat with Rabin would be cited in WADA's independent commission report on the Russian doping scandal. It was called an 'unsolicited meeting' where 'Director Rodchenkov stated he was operating in a system where he was forced to do things in his position. Director Rodchenkov would not elaborate what he was forced to do.' At least they didn't misquote me.

monitored every opening and closing of the freezer doors. Naturally, Blokhin's FSB experts had found a way to bypass this surveillance. and were able to swap urine samples in a five to ten-minute windows, with the monitors recording nothing. We were ready to begin our swapping sessions.

Next on the checklist was a test of our three-steroid Sochi cocktail. My subordinate-cum- bartender Aleksei Kuishkin mixed a massive batch of the 'soft' version of the cocktail, using vermouth rather than whisky as a base. Before drinking it, I urinated so I had a control sample, and then I sipped a few millilitres of our steroid mixture and swirled it around my mouth. I preferred my original Chivas Regal version, but never mind.

I tested the mixture for several days in a row, often chasing it with two cups of coffee and mint toothpaste to evade the ubiquitous post-holiday traffic checks by the Moscow police. Driving home on these cold winter nights sometimes took two hours, and I couldn't risk losing my licence. The upside was that nothing bad happened, but the downside was that when I arrived home, my bladder was close to bursting.

Let me explain what the now-notorious 'Duchess' cocktail could and could not do. Performance-enhancing anabolic steroids can benefit almost any athlete in almost any sport; the 'cocktail' was a fast-acting but low dose of three steroids, tailored to help athletes around the age of 30 recover after gruelling events. In many sports with preliminary heats or repeated races, rapid muscle recovery is the key to success.

The Sochi cocktail was specifically concocted to help veteran athletes like the long-distance skier Alexander Legkov, the biathlete Olga Zaitseva, the bobsledder Alexander Zubkov or the skeleton star Alexander Tretyakov. These competitors were perfectly prepared for the Olympic Games, but would not be able to recover from a gruelling day of competition as quickly as their younger rivals.

Let me re-emphasise that the 'Duchess' cocktail had nothing to do with preparing athletes for the Olympic Games. Proper preparation takes years, and it is this that makes you a medal winner. But the cocktail might make the difference between winning a gold or a bronze medal, helping you with that final, desperate kick that determines who will stand in which position on the podium.

Legkov won gold in the 50km cross-country ski race with a dramatic finishing burst; in previous years, without my cocktail, he had repeatedly lost in the final metres. Zubkov had a 0.07-second lead after four bobsled heats. In the skeleton, Tretyakov's margins were similar: during the month before the Olympics he improved his five-second burst of acceleration, when the athlete runs next to the sled before jumping in, by 0.05 of a second, and that was enough to win him a gold medal. So, yes, the cocktail made a significant difference to Russia's medal count.

In the meantime, Irina Rodionova was getting over-excited and acting as if she wanted to give the cocktail to any Russian athlete in Olympic uniform. I emphasised to her and to Nagornykh that we could switch ten bottles during our two hours of 'black ops' time each night, and no more. I told Nagornykh the same thing, and asked him for a list of who would be taking steroids during the Sochi Olympics. Of course, we could include only those

Irina Rodionova in my office, Moscow 2014.

athletes for whom we had verified, clean urine samples in Rodionova's CSP freezers. The day before I left for Sochi, I received the 'Duchess list' of 39 athletes. I discussed it with Irina, and insisted that we reduce the number to 36.

On 23 January I moved to Sochi for a two-month stay. Several days later, the shipment of clean urine arrived. Rodionova tried to get inside the Command Centre and organise the freezer storage, but she was unable to get past security. A few days later, Blokhin and I inspected the FSB Command Centre's freezers together. They were a mess. The clean urine was stored in soda bottles, jam jars and baby food containers, though the labelling was clear and written in permanent ink to prevent mix-ups. I had memorised the names of the 36 athletes in the steroid programme, and was surprised to discover a number of new names, such as the women's hockey team. I told Blokhin that we needed to create a reliable inventory and location map for all the samples, and he reluctantly agreed.

Athletes soon began to arrive in Sochi, and pre-competition doping control began on 31 January. On that day, the IOC tested the Russian biathletes, and the next day they tested the skiers – where doping was concerned, these were high-risk winter sports. Blokhin and I started our night-time swapping sessions. We were slightly nervous, but our conveyor belt seemed to work quite smoothly. On 2 February, my subordinate Yuri Chizhov arrived from Moscow and took over some of my swapping duties. He was a trained DCO, but helping us out at night would be his only job during the Games.

At the same time, I still had to fulfil my duties as laboratory director. We had 18 foreign experts in the laboratory, a list that had been agreed with WADA and the IOC. The experts, mostly PhDs and skilled researchers, were there to help us with the daily flood of analyses. In addition, the laboratory protocol, performance and operations were observed by four IOC representatives and one WADA observer, though they were not directly engaged in analysis. My colleague Thierry Boghosian, who knew every nook and cranny of our Moscow and Sochi laboratories, became our WADA-designated independent observer, responsible for daily oversight of our work.

Only Boghosian was allowed to come to the reception and storage area on the first floor at any hour of the day or night – I had granted him the same all-door access card that had been issued to me, my two secretaries, and Chizhov and Blokhin. All the other foreign experts had to remain on their assigned floors and left at around 6pm. Most of the samples were delivered at midnight and then all operations – registration, re-coding and aliquoting – were completed before the first shift came to work at 7am. It was the same protocol as had existed in London in 2012, with the addition of a parallel swapping session. We were as ready as we would ever be.

*

There was the usual scramble for tickets to the opening ceremony at the Fisht Olympic Stadium, the main Olympic arena, which was about a third of a mile away from the laboratory. We had arranged ten tickets for our 57 staffers and I secured four more, which I surrendered to my staff. Friends managed to find me two more tickets, but it turned out that my secretaries, accountants and quality control personnel had rifled through my desk and taken them all. In the end, like an estimated two billion people around the world, I watched the 7 February opening ceremony on TV, punctuated by frequent trips to the other side of the laboratory's fourth floor, which had a decent view of the stadium.

The flag-bearer Alexander Zubkov, a veteran bobsledder and one of the greatest cheats in Russian sports history, led the Russian team into the stadium and stood next to President Putin to watch the pageant, while I decided it was time to get some sleep. I collapsed on a couch in a private room of my large office, until Chizhov woke me up for a final check of our swapping routine.

I carefully measured the specific gravity of clean urine, poured the assigned volumes into rinsed A and B bottles and double-checked (or even triple-checked – Chizhov was monitoring my every move) the code numbers on the sanitised plastic caps and bottles. By 4 or 5am we were exhausted, but we had to avoid any mistakes. One by one, I sealed the B bottles, before Chizhov passed the A and B bottles through our 'mousehole' to the security zone where our storage freezers were located.

The first full night of the competition began ominously. Boghosian had flown in from Montreal and was suffering from jet lag, so he showed up in our laboratory at 1am and watched us collect the samples from the DCOs and register and re-code the bottles. It felt like he was lingering around the ground floor too long; luckily we weren't doing any large-scale swapping that night, just a couple of bottles, but his presence made Blokhin nervous, so he had his FSB team monitor Thierry's every move. Blokhin got advance notice of everything Thierry did; when his hotel door opened, when he booked a car, and so on.

The very next night after Thierry's midnight 'Hamlet's father's ghost' act turned out to be a sample-swapping extravaganza, and despite all our preparation, nothing seemed to go right. We had trouble processing the 'catch of the day', the bags full of samples arriving at the registration area; some documentation wasn't properly filled out and the paperwork was delayed. Then the FSB magicians in the next building had trouble opening several of the B bottles, and we began to get nervous. Poor Blokhin was shuttling back and forth to the Command Centre, trying to keep the assembly line on task. It turned out to be an exhausting, sleepless night, and I paid the price the next day – I felt weak, with no zest or energy.

During the early days of the Games, the WADA president

Sir Craig Reedie arrived to inspect the Olympic laboratory and proclaimed that he was very pleased with the foreign experts, with the visiting IOC professors and with my staff. The visit passed pleasantly, and everyone took photos and smiled to commemorate the occasion. But yet another echo from *Hamlet* had been rattling around in my head all day: I found myself imagining how Sir Craig would have reacted if he had known what we were doing at night. Doping control in Russia was truly 'out of joint', and neither WADA nor the IOC were 'born to set it right.'

WADA president Sir Craig Reedie (far right) inspects the Sochi Laboratory, with the laboratory personnel, 11 February 2014.

CHAPTER 4

'THE PIPES NEED FIXING AGAIN'

The first week of the Sochi Olympics was a big let-down for Team Russia. After seven days, we had only two gold medals, and neither of them was particularly praiseworthy. The first was a 'team trophy' for figure skating, a newly introduced category that had been added to please the host country. Our figure skating pair, Tatiana Volosozhar and Maxim Trankov, also won gold, but it felt like a partial victory because Tatiana was actually Ukrainian and had been drafted onto the Russian team after our pitiful showing at the Vancouver Games four years previously. After two more days without further golds, Viktor Ahn won the short track speed skating, but nor was that victory an entirely satisfying one. Ahn, a South Korean who had previously skated under the name Ahn Hyun-soo, won three medals in 2006. A world-class opportunist, he abandoned the South Korean team after a dispute over training conditions and went on to win several medals for his new 'homeland', but his victories didn't exactly feel Russian.

Finally, a 'real' Russian, Alexander Tretyakov, won gold in the skeleton. I gathered that he was a satisfied cocktail user when I received text messages and photos from Irina Rodionova of his doping control form right after he won his medal. I drove to the Azimut Hotel, where I found an anxious Irina. I calmed her down, assured her that our swapping plan would come off smoothly and then went to a convenience store to stock up on Bounty bars, Pepsi, ramen noodles, coffee and cigarettes to get my team through the night. Then we pulled an all-nighter, swapping out Tretyakov's urine in order to protect Russia's first true gold medal.

Contrary to what I had told Irina, the swapping didn't go smoothly at all. Seeing me taking notes, Blokhin became quite nervous, but of course I never mentioned the swapping in my diary. I did, however, write that he and Yuri Chizhov were 'running back

Waiting for delivery of the urine samples and preparing the night swapping session. In the meantime, Chizhov and Blokhin, and my secretaries, both called Anastasia, were watching TV in my office.

and forth and making noise' all night long, disturbing my naps in the operation room between swapping urine in the BEREG-kit bottles.

Another disappointment in the first week, besides the lack of gold medals, was that no athletes were caught doping – we had a gleaming, state-of-the-art doping control laboratory and no scalps to show for it! We did detect several positive results, but none of them amounted to a doping case – they were what WADA would call adverse analytical findings (AAFs) but were disregarded because the athletes had therapeutic use exemptions (TUEs) that allowed them to use corticosteroids and asthma medications.

The other positives were double-blind samples (DBs), urine samples containing prohibited substances that the IOC Medical Commission planted from time to time to check a laboratory's performance. Those DBs were easily detectable because they contained ridiculous compounds like diuretic metolazone, which was never seen in doping control routine analysis, or fluoxymesterone, an anabolic steroid from the 1980s that was also extremely rare in doping – only four cases had been reported during the past four years. I was disappointed. I had promised my friends Christiane Ayotte and Martial Saugy that we would find ten positives, and so far we hadn't found any.

As the Games went on, we began to uncover genuine anti-doping rule violations. The first victim was the German biathlete Evi Sachenbacher-Stehle, who had small amounts of methylhexanamine in her urine after a race. Hers was a borderline case; this stimulant usually occurred in huge concentrations, so it was up to me whether to report her result as an AAF or not. If I had already logged five genuine AAFs, representing anti-doping rule violations, before coming across Evi's sample, I might not have turned her in. But because of the drought of positives, we needed blood so reported that one.

Before reporting Evi, I checked her doping control form to see which sport nutrition and medicines she had declared. I could tell she wasn't a Russian team member and Irina hadn't texted me her code number, so we dropped the hammer and she was banned from competition. A huge scandal erupted, and when she showed up for her B sample analysis, Hajo Seppelt, a German documentary filmmaker, camped out in front of our laboratory with a cameraman, hoping to get some footage of Evi. Unfortunately the car that brought her through our gates had tinted windows, so Hajo missed out on a scoop.

I felt bad for Evi. The punishment didn't really fit her crime, a borderline doping violation, but her case opened the door for further findings. The IOC eventually announced eight positives during the last five days of the Games, and each day we staged a ceremonial opening of the B bottles in the presence of the athletes and various officials. So we got our scalps. At a dinner on 22 February, a group of high-level IOC and WADA dignitaries called us the best Olympic laboratory ever! If they only knew . . .

I remember watching a live broadcast of the men's 4x10km biathlon relay, which Russia won. One biathlete, Alexander Loginov, wasn't on the team because at the end of 2013 the Cologne laboratory had placed a hold on his urine sample; it looked like an EPO positive, but they couldn't confirm it using their current methodology.

However, they knew that a new methodology was going to be introduced in 2014, and that it would probably result in an AAF that would become reportable after the Olympic Games. It was a particularly complex case because Loginov's urine sample revealed both endogenous (natural) and exogenous (injected) EPO. I had been shown the results; had I not informed the Russian biathlon team about it, Loginov would have been competing in the 4x7.5km Men's Relay in Sochi, and Russia might have lost a gold medal following his retrospective disqualification. That was one occasion when I was proud of my assistance[5].

The closing ceremony was on 23 February, but yet again I didn't have tickets. However, I was happy and slept well in the laboratory, despite the noise and music blaring from the stadium next door. We had our last important swapping session to protect two gold medals, the first won by Alexander Legkov in the 50-kilometre skiing event and the second by the four-man bobsled driven by Alexander Zubkov. I joked that they were having their closing ceremony in the stadium, and we were having our own final 'closing ceremony', sealing the last tampered B bottles from the Sochi Games. It felt like a mirror image of two different Olympics.

---

5 On February 15 2020, it was announced that Evgeny Ustyugov, a member of the men's relay team, was disqualified in retrospect: his urine sample dated 29 August 2013 contained oxandrolone long-term metabolites. As such, his gold medal in the biathlon relay was annulled, and the Russian Federation lost first place in the overall medal table to Norway. Canada became second, and Russia dropped to third.

Finally, the Olympics Games was over. The magicians would be going home and we would never have to swap another B bottle in the Sochi laboratory. We packed up 80 boxes of blood and urine samples and sent them all to Lausanne, for what the IOC call the 'repatriation of athletes' samples'. Then we celebrated the end of the Games in our favourite restaurant, Laluna, drinking, dancing and singing karaoke. We would all have a headache tomorrow, guaranteed.

My diary entry for 24 February reads as follows: 'The Olympic Games are over, the currency went up, revolution in Ukraine – damn.'

*

We had no plans to swap samples during the upcoming Paralympics; yet again, I fell back on my favourite Donna Summer song, 'Enough is Enough'. How naïve of me.

In contrast to the Olympic Games, the Paralympics were quiet and relaxing, like a jog to cool down after a strenuous three-mile race. Now that the 'real' Olympic Games were over, we were no longer on high alert. RUSADA staff resumed the ordinary delivery of samples from Russian competitions and training camps around the country, and we performed routine analyses as we would have back home in Moscow.

The Paralympic Games started on 7 March and continued without incident until we began to detect numerous positive results among Russian gold medal winners. Specifically, we were finding trimetazidine (Preductal), a common stimulant widely used in the former Eastern Bloc. WADA and the International

Paralympic Committee (the IPC) had added it to their 'Prohibited List' in 2014, but it seemed that the Russian Paralympic athletes hadn't been informed of the change.

We hadn't received any kind of warning or heads-up, so we analysed the dirty samples as we would any others. There were no foreign experts or observers left in the Sochi laboratory, so on-site discovery wouldn't be a problem. However, what *would* be a problem was that the IPC had decided that we should transfer all the samples to Lausanne after the Games, for long-term storage and reanalysis, which meant we would have to swap out the dirty samples. To make matters worse, Russian parathletes continued to win gold medals in skiing and biathlon and every other new gold medal came accompanied by a positive urine sample.

Russian parathletes and their coaches were eligible for the same perks given to able-bodied Olympic champions, meaning cash bounties of tens of thousands of dollars, new cars, desirable apartments, access to foreign training camps and so on. The stakes were just as high as in the regular Olympic Games – for them and for us. We needed to keep these medals in Russia where they belonged.

I told Evgeny Blokhin that the situation was getting out of hand, and that we needed to summon the magicians back to Sochi. Using Aesopian language, I wrote the following in my diary, making reference to Blokhin pretending to be a plumber: 'We're deciding with Evgeny Ivanovich what to do with the water pipes. The pipes need fixing again – it's time to call in the brigade.'

The magicians had earned plenty of holiday from all those nights shifts in Sochi, and it took Deputy Minister Nagornykh two days to gather them. This time, because the foreign observers had left, we performed the swapping during the daytime. We kept the magicians in Sochi for another three days, until the end of the Paralympic Games, and did the final swap on 15 March. Things were pretty quiet by this time, so I asked Chizhov to run the session – he had plenty of experience by now. The only problem was where the clean urine would come from – I couldn't remember pre-testing any 'clean urine' from the parathletes in 2013.[6]

On 15 March, I wrote in my diary: 'We completed the deal with Blokhin – George Antilsky delivered the lemonade.' This meant that Blokhin and I were waiting for Evgeny Antilsky, manager of the doping control station, to deliver the clean urine for the swapping session. Irina Rodionova was the person who came up with all these funny nicknames, such as 'magicians', 'Duchess' and 'lemonade'.

We received our last samples on 17 March and sent them all to Lausanne on 19 March. The Sochi laboratory was finally closed. I hadn't had a day off or seen one live event during the Olympics or the Paralympics – my staff had hoovered up every ticket and invitation that arrived in my office, but I didn't begrudge them.

---

6 The principal difference here was that the urine swapping took place *after* the laboratory analysis – there was no time pressure and less need for secrecy. Another difference was that the washed A and B BEREG-kit bottles sat in the laboratory for several days, waiting for the clean urine to be delivered. The trimetazidine positives were completely unexpected.

I flew from Sochi to Lisbon for a meeting of WADA laboratory directors. President Reedie presented me with a signed copy of the updated World Anti-Doping Code and I gave a talk about our laboratory work in Sochi – omitting certain details, of course.

From Lisbon I flew on to Cologne, for my beloved Manfred Donike Workshop on doping control in sport. It was the 32nd annual meeting – 19 of them having been held since Manfred's untimely death – and I delivered the inaugural lecture, which was on 'Doping Control during the Olympic Games in Sochi.'

I then flew back to Moscow, where I witnessed the final inspection of our laboratory by WADA's independent quality management experts. They gave us a clean bill of health, concluding that our laboratory 'assured accurate anti-doping testing results, within the scope of WADA accreditation.' WADA accepted their conclusions and the threatened six-month suspension of our accreditation never happened. This marked the end of the nightmarish 18-month-long WADA investigation.

It was a great victory! Ever since the FSKN first came after me in 2011, I had been on the receiving end of one investigation or another. I definitely wasn't as pure as the driven snow, but the WADA wrecking crew, with their half-baked 'tips' from second-tier whistle-blowers and Russian troublemakers, never really knew what they were looking for, and consistently tried to label me as a money-grubbing kingpin. Which I was not. I felt happy for my staff and for myself – I could finally resume my job in peace, or so I thought.

*

My year-long rental of the Sochi laboratory building was due to expire on 30 April 2014, so we spent the last two days of the month making an inventory of the building's contents, before handing it back to the owner. Somehow an extra table and wardrobe had materialised and three chairs had gone missing. There was also a huge mountain of rubbish outside the building. I agreed to pay for its removal, and in return we didn't have to justify the furniture discrepancy. For some reason Yuri Chizhov got very drunk and aggressive with me, badgering me about why we should have to pay for the garbage outside our building to be collected.

You can fall in love with 'things', and I was definitely in love with that laboratory building. I'd loved our hectic days, the noise of the instruments, the shared enthusiasm and the non-stop laughter. Our foreign visitors always seemed to be surprised that we were having so much fun at work. Now the building was empty and we would never relive those days again.

Looking at the inebriated Chizhov, I realised that I should do something weird. I went to the aliquotting and secret operation rooms and started taking photos of the 'mousehole' and the adjacent doors to Rooms 124 and 125. Chizhov sobered up a little then, and seemed nervous. What did I think I was doing, he asked. This was completely against the rules.

I told him that the Ministry of Sport had ordered me to document our experience.

Now that it was all over, I felt desolate. I had spent a year and a half of my life here. It had left me exhausted, and I was unable

The infamous 'mousehole' from Operational Room 124.

to stop repeating my friend Christiane Ayotte's favourite catch-phrase, 'Please leave me alone.'

I had loved Sochi's sky, sun, seashore and mountains, but that day was cloudy with gusts of wind and rain. The weather was gloomy; it was impossible not to feel pessimistic.

CHAPTER 5

STORM IS THREATENING

The summer of 2014 was the 'Summer of Fateful Meetings', which jolted me out of my post-Sochi contentment. In June, I received a call from the German documentary filmmaker Hajo Seppelt, who I had known since my trial by fire in Johannesburg eight months earlier. He covered the international sport doping scene closely, and though he affected the shambolic attitude of someone who wanted you to think he wasn't sure what he was looking into, Hajo was quite well organised and kept his eye on the ball.

Hajo disdained WADA as a hot air machine, which matched my own views. His countryman Thomas Bach, a former Olympic gold medal fencer, was the newly appointed president of the IOC, and Hajo wasn't wild about him either. He and I had chatted quite a bit in the corridors of the WADA conference in Johannesburg, and he had filmed our laboratory in Sochi during routine media appearances. He had been desperate to see the opening of Evi Sachenbacher-Stehle's B sample in Sochi, but of course we couldn't let him in.

Hajo convinced me that German TV was finishing a special report about the success of the Sochi Olympics, focusing on the unique atmosphere, the beautiful venues and the unforgettable memories. He intended to single out my laboratory for praise, but needed more realistic footage than the shots we had permitted during the Games. He was aware that I'd taken all the instrumentation back to Moscow, and said he would be deeply indebted to me if I'd let him film some scenes in the laboratory at the Moscow ADC. He also wanted me to explain yet again how doping control had succeeded so marvellously at the Russian Games.

Should I have smelled a rat? In any case, I cleared the meeting with Deputy Minister Nagornykh, who approved Hajo's visit. After all, he hadn't made any trouble for us in Sochi, and there was no reason to think he would start now.

Hajo and I agreed to meet at the ADC the next day. As usual, I had been putting out various fires – The weightlifters! The race walkers! The biathletes! – so I was functioning on just a couple of hours of sleep. I had no reason to fear him and his crew, but he was planning to stage an ambush.

His cameraman had been filming some of our equipment, while I was talking about analytical and technical issues. Then there was a pause while the cameraman moved to the opposite corner of the room, and I sat down on a laboratory stool. Suddenly, Hajo asked me a question: 'Have you ever accepted money to cover up doping?'

I was dumbfounded. Had I fallen asleep while someone switched the subject of our talk?

The context for his question was that he had interviewed

several Russian athletes and coaches who had accused me of running a corporate fee-for-service cheating machine that extorted huge sums of money from competitors, in return for 'clean' doping tests. Some of these whistle-blowers were the people who tried to interest WADA in the doping shenanigans of Russian athletes, with mixed results.

I wasn't running an extortion ring, much less a multi-million-rouble one, but I was nonetheless taken aback by his question. I hesitated for a long time before answering, and when I finally managed to deny his allegation, my arms were tightly crossed over my chest defensively and I was looking at the floor. The optics were bad, to put it mildly.

When I'd gathered my thoughts, I explained to Hajo that if I had been taking money to whitewash positive results, there would be queues of Russian athletes outside the laboratory after every major competition, eager to pay for my services. Moreover, athletes who were doping would be happy to pay me in advance, to assure negative results in future.

I had no idea at the time how he would use our brief exchange, but it was clear that he wasn't preparing a puff piece about our successes in Sochi.

Just a few days later, on 17 July, I escaped Moscow to attend the International Sport Science Symposium at the University of Oregon in Eugene, a famous American running centre. While waiting for a connection in Amsterdam, I noticed several groups of Malaysians mingling in the duty-free shops. A few hours later they would all be dead; a Russian missile launched from Ukraine struck Malaysia Airlines Flight MH17, bound for Kuala

Lumpur, killing 298 people. During the next three days in Eugene, I watched the TV reports about what President Barack Obama called an 'outrage of unspeakable proportions'.

The symposium took place just across the street from Hayward Field, the stadium where the distance runner Steve Prefontaine used to compete. Two days into my trip, I asked the organisers to drive me to the scene of his death. After a short drive, I found myself standing in front of the polished stone memorial to 'Pre', at the hairpin bend where he lost his life in a car accident in May 1975. Prefontaine was one of the most influential distance runners who ever lived and a huge influence on my life as a runner, along with the Ukrainian Vladimir Kuts, the 5,000 and 10,000-metre world record holder and double Olympic champion in Melbourne in 1956.[7] I remember reading in Prefontaine's brief obituary in *Sovietsky Sport* that he was the US record holder for all distance races between 2,000 and 10,000 metres. The highlight of his career was his famous loss in the 5,000 metres at the 1972 Munich Olympic Games to the Finnish star Lasse Viren.[8] I recall seeing photos of Prefontaine in that race, his bushy moustache and long black hair flowing while he

7 When I was communicating with the FSB I sometimes had to use a pseudonym, and I always chose 'Kuts'.

8 It might seem strange to call a loss the 'highlight' of a runner's career. In the famous race, Viren simply had more gas in the tank than Pre in the final lap. Viren had also run the heat and final of the 10,000 metres, as well as the heat and the semi-final for the 5,000 metres; by the time the final came around, he was exhausted compared to Pre, who hadn't competed in the 10,000 metres. However, after Palestinian terrorists murdered Israeli athletes in Munich, a day of mourning was declared, which gave Viren an extra day to recover.

ran like the wind. When I was a junior runner I loved to lead the pack, just like Pre did, until a new coach taught me the tactic of the sit-and-kick, and the 'negative split', when you run the second half of a race faster than the first.

When Russian society became more open, I was able to devour books about Prefontaine and watched his races and interviews on YouTube. That famous memorial at the place where he died was a place I had always dreamed of visiting.

Eugene was also the site of my first encounter with the American filmmaker Bryan Fogel. A champion amateur cyclist, he wanted to make a movie explaining how the Tour de France champion Lance Armstrong was able to dope for so many years and win so many titles, without being caught. Fogel recruited me to be his personal 'witch doctor'. He intended to name his documentary *Icarus* because he wanted to fly high in the cycling world using a bespoke doping programme, developed with my assistance.

Don Catlin, the former director of the UCLA Olympic Analytical Laboratory, had referred Bryan to me, probably because he didn't want to lend his name to the enterprise. But I was up for anything. I didn't accept any payments from Bryan, but I accepted the project because, to be honest, life had become boring. The Sochi Olympics were behind me, we seemed to have shooed away the WADA monster and the movie sounded like fun.

At the time, Bryan was a one-man band, a filmmaker who carried his own camera and tripod with him. He had prepared three pages of tightly compiled questions for our first interview on 21 July, many of them about the greatest doped cyclist of all time. If Lance Armstrong had been tested hundreds of time over 15 years, why were the results always negative? I explained to Bryan that that was par for the course; doping control laboratories report thousands of false negative results each year.

Here is my diary entry for 21 July 2014, the day I met Bryan:

'Went to the Nike store, nothing to buy, couldn't find any sneakers. Had some beer, returned to the hotel. Raining (of course) they wouldn't let us into the stadium to film, so we went into the law school and recorded for two hours. We discussed everything, but he has *kasha* in his brain [it means that he's confused about some of the issues]. We went to the bar, drank whisky and beer, and chatted.'

*

Back in Moscow, I received some strange news: Vladimir Putin had chosen me and Irina Rodionova as recipients of the Order of Friendship, a coveted state honour. With this award, you get access to special medical care and discounted apartments, and the benefits extend to your widow. Nagornykh called to congratulate me; it was a happy occasion, because the criminal investigation in 2011 had prevented me from receiving a state award after the 2012 London Games. Now, after Sochi, it had finally happened!

Putin planned to present the awards at the beginning of October, but I had a prior commitment to attend a USADA conference in Tempe, Arizona. At the same time, my 82-year-old father was seriously ill. Should I go to the US, I asked him, or should I stay here, receive the award from Putin and take care of you?

'You're a scientist, Putin is a jerk and I'll still be alive when you get back,' he assured me. I informed the Kremlin that I would shortly be leaving for a conference in the US and they removed my name from the guestlist. One of my father's statements proved to be untrue: he died while I was in Arizona and I arranged his funeral when I returned from the US.

Having arrived back in Moscow, I was summoned to the Ministry of Sport to accept my award. I assumed I would be receiving an Order of Friendship for the Sochi Games, since I had missed the Kremlin ceremony while I was in the US, but instead they gave me a Presidential Award for the London Games in 2012! At the State Museum of Sport, Minister Mutko handed me an honorary diploma, signed by President Putin, for my 'indispensable contribution to the success of the XXX Olympic Games in London'.

My diary entry for that day read, 'Where is my Order of Friendship?' Ironically, I would receive that award a few months later, when I was well on my way to becoming Russia's public enemy number one, but that was a turn of events no one could have foreseen.

*

Now came the bombshell. On 22 November 2014, I received a letter from Hajo Seppelt explaining that ARD Television was putting the finishing touches to a shocking documentary about doping in Russian sport. The next day ARD sent an official letter, in English, with a series of questions accusing me of extorting money from athletes and concealing positive cases. It read:

> German TV ARD is producing a TV report about alleged doping practices in Russia. We kindly ask you to answer the following questions concerning this topic so that we

can accurately present your point of view. To do so, please answer no later than Thursday, 27 November 2014.

1. According to our research, you provided access or even sold prohibited substances to athletes or third parties, e.g., coaches. By order or initiative of whom did you do so?

2. According to our research, you advised athletes concerning the use of prohibited substances and methods. By order or initiative of whom did you do so?

3. According to our information, you declared 'negative' doping test results which in fact were 'positive' or otherwise helped in the cover-up of doping tests. Is this correct? If so, did you act, in one or more cases, corresponding to monetary payments or other benefits? And by order or initiative of whom did you do so?

4. In 2011 you were under criminal investigation under the subject of illegal steroid storage and distribution. Did you face criminal charges and what was the outcome?'

My childhood friend and occasional rival, Dr Nikita Kamaev, head of RUSADA, received a similar letter. My diary entry for that day reads, 'I called Yuri Nagornykh to warn him that a storm was coming.' I knew he would know exactly what I meant.

I answered the ARD letter, denying everything, and Nikita did the same. Lying and denying was to be expected at our level of the food chain, where we were responsible for collecting samples and analysing results. Above us, the bureaucrats and functionaries were making noise, obfuscating with the best of

them and even making threats. Above them stood the IOC and
WADA, with their airy talk about the 'integrity of sport'.

I couldn't lie to my diary, and wrote on 22 November: 'They
want answers to some very ugly questions. I briefed Nagornykh.'

Nagornykh seemed to know what the documentary was going
to say, and even the scheduled transmission date: 3 December.
Maybe he was just bluffing, because by the time that date rolled
around, he seemed nervous and disoriented.

A group of us, including Nagornykh, gathered at the Pano-
rama television studio in the Novosti news agency building
to watch the documentary as it was transmitted, at 10pm in
Moscow. The Russian sports broadcaster Vasily Kiknadze had
arranged for a simultaneous translation irrigated with French
cognac, so we kept quiet and listened to the Russian and German
versions at the same time.

My diary for that evening notes that I wore a suit for the occasion and that we enjoyed a well-stocked bar. 'Nagornykh is on a
trigger's edge,' I wrote. 'The ARD is planning a documentary
about the doping mafia, DDR style in Russia.' (The East Ger-
mans operated an impressive state-sponsored doping operation
in their heyday.)

The documentary was a damning indictment of many different
characters in the Russian doping establishment, primarily
Dr Sergey Portugalov, the athletics boss Valentin Balakhnichev, the
coach Alexey Melnikov and, to a lesser extent, me. Hajo wrapped
his somewhat scattershot tale of doping chicanery in Russia around
the telegenic young Stepanov couple: the American-educated Vitaly, who had worked as a low-level staffer at RUSADA, and his

wife Yuliya, a runner whose career had never quite taken off. She had been busted for doping and clearly had an axe to grind.

It turned out the Stepanovs had been writing letters to WADA for several years, urging them to investigate the 'Russian doping scandal'. With the exception of the 2013 raid on the ADC, WADA had generally ignored them, but Hajo didn't.

My on-camera performance was weak, but Nikita Kamaev had allowed Hajo to film in his office and forcefully denied every allegation. Some of Hajo's evidence didn't seem convincing, because he'd had trouble contacting the affected athletes. The revelations about hundred-thousand-euro wire transfers to and from a shell company in Singapore didn't look good, but they were Balakhnichev's shady deals, so they were his problem.

I noted in my diary that 'the main hit landed on Balakhnichev, who was accused of charging [Russian marathon runner Liliya] Shobukhova 400,000 euros. They weaved in some footage of [discus thrower Evgeniya] Pecherina yapping against me. I drove home carefully.' In Moscow, you always drive home carefully after an evening out, because the traffic police are extremely vigilant and will confiscate your driver's licence at the merest suggestion of a whiff of cognac.

Hajo's documentary flailed around various subjects, but while it certainly cast a cloud of suspicion over Russian sport, I thought I would survive it. I kept expecting them to say something horrible about me – about the swapping at Sochi, for instance – but the crescendo never really came. I didn't look great, but my main accuser was Yuliya Stepanova, a has-been runner I had never met and from whom I had never 'extorted' anything. With only five minutes left in the documentary, I knew I was in the clear and could breathe freely again. Balakhnichev was the enemy and I hadn't dealt with him in years. The Stepanovs were the enemy but I hardly knew them. I had received presidential citations, and Vitaly Mutko had protected me from bigger shitstorms than this. I would survive.

That conclusion was reinforced the following day, when a group of us – me, Mutko, Nagornykh, Kamaev, Professor Ramil Khabriev from RUSADA and Natalya Zhelanova, Mutko's 'doping control adviser' – gathered in a small conference room next to Mutko's office to watch the documentary again. Those of us who had seen the film before were sniggering and joking around – no one thought much would come of these random accusations. But I wasn't there to watch the film – I was there to observe Mutko, who was watching for the first time. He remained impassive, though he did make a joke at my expense, noticing that I 'paused as if I were a character in a Chekhov play' when Hajo sprang his surprise question on me.

Mutko thought that Balakhnichev might not survive the accusations against him, but otherwise didn't seem too perturbed. I pointed out that all the whistle-blowers were athletes whose careers had already ended when they were disqualified for doping. 'As long as they weren't getting caught, they kept their mouths shut,' I noted, to the general approval of my colleagues.

What would we do? Nothing, Mutko decided. We would issue no official statement and offer no interviews. Hajo Seppelt was promising two more episodes, so Mutko decided to keep our powder dry until all the facts were in.

*

The follow-up to Hajo's *The Secrets of Doping: How Russia Makes its Winners*, which aired a few days later, was unremarkable and pretty much a rehash of the first episode. Maybe, just like every previous time the international doping authorities had decided to 'nail' the Russians, we would emerge unscathed. Hajo's sources were disgruntled ex-dopers and his 'evidence', for the most part, consisted of grainy surreptitious phone recordings of conversations that would certainly never be admissible in any serious adjudication process.

Perhaps we talked ourselves into believing that we had slipped the noose. No such luck.

On 10 December, a week after the documentary aired, the WADA scientific director Dr Olivier Rabin sent me a letter and demanded that I acknowledge receipt in writing. I should mention that when Hajo had interviewed Rabin for his film, he had offered some cutting comments on the Russian anti-doping scene, noting how positive results had a tendency to disappear in certain circumstances. This was what Richard McLaren would in 2016 sardonically call the 'disappearing positive methodology'.

'Do you mean corruption?' Hajo asked.

'Interference' was the word Olivier preferred. 'There may be interference.'

Olivier's letter asked for two mutually exclusive things. Referring to the International Standard for Laboratories (ISL), WADA urged me to retain all A and B samples kept in Moscow, but in the next sentence he referred to a specific paragraph in the ISL rules that required samples be retained for three months, in our case starting from 10 September.

I knew Rabin was ordering me to preserve *all* samples, but this confusion was a godsend for my defence. When we got his letter, the ADC had 13,000 frozen samples dating back to April, when we had moved back from Sochi. We knew we had plenty of positives that had been reported as negatives. Our swapping operation had affected a tiny percentage of Russian athletes – generally Olympic champions and medal winners.

We hadn't bothered to tamper with most samples, because they belonged to junior 'rising stars', to local Moscow athletes or to nobodies, so they didn't matter. After misreporting as negatives, the International Standard for Laboratories allowed us to dispose of them after 90 days.

The bad news was that Rabin's demand was being made in the name of an ad hoc independent commission (IC), formed to investigate allegations made in the ARD documentary and chaired by former WADA president Dick Pound. The IC intended to come to Moscow and turn our laboratory upside down, yet again.

The good news was that the ambiguity in Rabin's letter gave us an opportunity to eliminate all our samples received between April and 10 September, and that is exactly what we did.

In addressing this possibly calamitous demand, we were blessed with some extraordinary luck that completely eliminated the possibility of a surprise inspection. WADA demanded an urgent visa for Rabin and his team to arrive in Moscow on Monday 15 December, which gave us the whole weekend to prepare. Then the Ministry of Sport said they couldn't issue a visa until Tuesday, so taking into account the time difference with Montreal,

Rabin and his allies would get to Moscow by Tuesday evening at the earliest. That gave us enough days to prepare.

The next day I switched off my telephones and took some time to consider what we would have to hide and swap out before WADA showed up. We had almost ten thousand paired samples, the most problematic being 56 samples from the National Weightlifting Championships in Grozny in August. The weightlifters' urine included 23 positives, as well as unnatural steroid profiles. We could never swap those out; we would have to make them disappear. Rabin's letter asking for samples dated after 10 September allowed us to do that.

Autumn was a quiet season for competitive sport, so I calculated that we 'only' had to clean up 37 positive samples. If it had been mid-summer, we might have had 100 positives; 37 might be manageable. Nikita Kamaev took seven samples belonging to professional boxers from Podolsk off my hands, which was a start.

We had the weekend to work with. I reported our calculations to Nagornykh on Friday morning, 12 December; he promised to do his best to send some experienced magicians to open bottles, and they appeared in the laboratory the very same day. Within five hours they had carefully opened 30 B bottles, with no visible damage, cracks or scratches – they hadn't lost the Sochi touch! I ordered borscht and chicken for them from a nearby Ukrainian restaurant, opened the best cognac from the bar in my office, and we all enjoyed a late lunch.

Friday was a long day. I drove back home at around 10pm, and then Mutko called me. He advised me to stay strong and firm and wished me the best of luck for the next few days.

This was going to be much more complicated than the Sochi operation. There, we knew which athletes to look out for and we had a fully stocked supply of clean urine, which we could substitute into their A and B bottles before the laboratory analysis. Here, we had already logged their steroid profiles into ADAMS, misreporting some positives as negatives, but we didn't have clean urine to swap into the A and B bottles, and we didn't even know all the athletes involved. We had to select useable urine samples from the thousands we hand on hand, being careful to match up the donor's steroid profile and specific gravity. The DNA of the swapped samples wouldn't correspond to the original, but we had no choice.

This would be a very tricky operation. We were all tired, nervous, and petrified of mismatching the coded caps of the A and B bottles – obvious evidence of tampering. It never happened, but I was still paranoid. Upon closer examination, we realised that nine of our positives contained such tiny amounts of ostarine, GW1516 and steroids that we could prove they had fallen beneath our detection limits. We ended up swapping 21 urine samples and I think we resealed the other nine with no manipulation, though my memory isn't clear and I may have added a bit of distilled water and salt to further decrease the concentration of foreign substances.

The rest of the bottles were disposed of in the old-fashioned way: we arranged for a rubbish truck to come and take thousands of samples to a landfill 30 kilometres outside Moscow, having filled two huge containers with BEREG-kit bottles – several tons of glass and urine that we were happy to see the back of!

Another problem we faced was that the false negatives could still be discovered in our laboratory documentation. It was hell to have to rewrite all this, but my assistant Evgeny Kudryavtsev got it done, in some cases falsifying the signatures of personnel who no longer worked at the ADC. This process took us into Tuesday, but, combined with the 'golden hands' of the veteran magicians, it looked like we had met our deadline and could survive an inspection. The timing was perfect; on Tuesday 16 December, Rabin phoned me from Paris to tell me to expect him at the laboratory the following morning. We were ready.

Olivier arrived with Victoria Ivanova and Thierry Boghosian, as well as blue plastic boxes in which to pack up all our urine samples. After they'd inspected our storage documents, Olivier asked what had happened to the samples belonging to the seven boxes, and I explained that they'd been forwarded to RUSADA. However, when he discovered that we'd sent thousands of samples to the dump, he went ballistic.

Rabin and I discussed our mass disposal of samples the next morning. We'd scheduled the disposal well in advance, I told him – knowing that garbage trucks were not permitted to enter Moscow city limits on workdays, we had taken advantage of the final weekend before the New Year holidays to get rid of our backlog.

'What about the letter?' Olivier asked. 'WADA wanted you to retain *all* samples! Wasn't that clear?'

'Yes,' I answered. 'But then the letter specified retaining the samples collected after 10 September. I disposed of the 1,417 samples to minimise your hunting area. I had to protect my laboratory.' I didn't mention that we had thrown away 8,200 paired samples!

He was livid, and documented our exchange for use in the eventual IC report.[9] When he said he wanted to retrieve all the bottles that had been sent to the dump, I explained that the dump was in a security zone, and entry without permission was forbidden. Anyway, the samples would by now be buried under tons of new garbage.

After two days of hard work, 26 boxes were ready for shipment to Lausanne, each weighing over a hundred pounds and containing 224 bottles. The shipment totalled 2,912 paired A and B samples. Rabin wanted to send our bottles to Cologne – I think he worried that my friend Martial Saugy in Lausanne might be too sympathetic towards me – but the laboratory there didn't have sufficient storage capacity.

It took me a week to prepare the documentation for the 'repatriation' of samples to Lausanne, but then we encountered another delay because TNT didn't have big enough refrigerator trucks available. Only on 26 December did the fateful cargo finally leave the Anti-Doping Centre. The future looked very murky.

9 'On 10 December 2014, WADA received an email from Director Rodchenkov, stating "this is to confirm the receipt of the OR [Olivier Rabin] Letter regarding sample storage in Moscow Anti-Doping Centre." That same day, Director Rodchenkov sent a second email to Dr Rabin, stating, "everything is working, your Letter received OK, samples are securely kept, the whole collection."'

CHAPTER 6

THE SECRET POLICE DESERVE THE TRUTH

On 21 January 2015, Mutko and Nagornykh summoned me to an urgent meeting. Mutko knew there was trouble brewing with forthcoming disqualifications for abnormal changes to the athlete biological passport, and wanted me to write up a quick overview that would help him explain the situation to the media and the apparatchiks.

At the same time, an old friend of mine in the FSB asked me for a straightforward first-hand explanation, so I drafted a six-page memo assessing the Russian doping scene for a top-level FSB audience. This was the unvarnished truth, and it wasn't a very pretty picture. I'm an organiser by nature, so I addressed our collective concerns:

1. How did we get into this mess?

   Ironically, organisations like the IOC and the IAAF would be happy to see the 'doping scandals' disappear because they're bad for business. But the media, especially

ARD in Germany but also many other news outlets, smelled blood. The athletes' defence lawyer Alexander Chebotarev got the ball rolling with his juicy 2013 leak to the *Daily Mail* that appeared just before the World Universiade and IAAF World Championships, two major sporting events held in Russia in 2013. Now the press had plenty more informants: the Stepanovs and their ilk.

2. An assessment of the threat

Two major events loomed before us. First, if the media applied enough pressure, the IOC would have to reanalyse athletes' test samples from the 2008 Beijing Olympics and they would inevitably target the Russians. We were the big doping story; no one else mattered.

I anticipated that this would result in ten positives in track and field and ten more in weightlifting. Separately, I thought, biological passport analysis would disqualify at least five more of Chegin's race walkers prior to the Rio Games in 2016.

On a positive note, I thought Martial Saugy in Lausanne might give us a heads-up if and when the IOC started rooting around in the Beijing samples that were stored in his laboratory, but I never discussed that with him.

Worse news for us was the fact that from January 2016, the IOC would have the right to test any Russian Olympian anywhere they chose. Two new German testing companies were replacing the hopelessly compromised Swedish firm IDTM, which meant that there would be two companies operating in

Russia, prepared at any moment to collect a sample from any Russian athlete unannounced and send it abroad.

In regards to the forthcoming Olympic Games in Rio, I inserted the fateful words 'and all the successful experience gained in Sochi can no longer be used'. I was making the point here that we could probably never again get away with the kind of in-laboratory swapping we had performed in Sochi. This little clause set off alarm bells everywhere and resulted in my report being classified 'Top Secret', which meant that not even Mutko could read it!

Mutko knew about the swapping, of course, though not from me: when Blokhin first demonstrated successful bottle tampering to me in February 2013, Nagornykh informed Mutko immediately, but he and I never communicated directly about the FSB magicians. I was allowed to discuss the swapping only with Nagornykh, Blokhin, Rodionova, Chizhov and Kudryavtsev, and never with anyone else – not with coaches nor athletes, and not with Mutko, Kamaev, or Sobolevsky. No competitor ever knew what went on in Room 124 in Sochi, although some might have had their suspicions. After all, why had we collected so much clean urine from them in the months before the Games? And why were they instructed to close their BEREG-kit bottles without fully tightening the screw caps, and then immediately report their code numbers and provide photos of their doping control forms?

My report ended with a prediction that turned out to be quite wrong: I told the secret police that if we could obstruct a reanalysis of the stored Olympic samples in Lausanne, WADA's

Independent Committee 'won't do anything single-handedly – they don't have the experience or the resources'. I made this statement based on a conversation that Mutko reported with WADA president Sir Craig Reedie. Reedie was friends with Natalia Zhelanova and had confided that he just wanted this whole Russia headache to go away.

In my report, I pointed out that I had beaten off one WADA investigation, in Johannesburg, and there was no reason to think that we could elude WADA's grasp again. However, that is not quite what happened.

*

27 February 2015 was a dark day in my life. I was negotiating the weekend traffic jams while listening to an hour-long interview with Boris Nemtsov on the Echo Moscow radio station. Just a few hours later, they announced that Nemtsov had been shot on the Bolshoi Moskvoretsky Bridge – the very same bridge I'd driven under every day for ten years, just 200 metres from the walls of the Kremlin.

I spent the next day in a depressed funk, just trying to imagine how Nemtsov could have been assassinated. Born in Sochi, he had become one of the brightest stars in modern Russia. Handsome and forward-looking, he was a protégé of Boris Yeltsin, who served as deputy prime minister at the beginning of the Putin era, before becoming an opposition politician and publishing numerous books about corruption and the increasing chaos in Russia.

A PhD physicist by training, Nemtsov had a wicked sense of humour and once remarked that by holding the Winter Olympics in Sochi, Russia had 'found one of the only places where there is no snow in the winter. Sochi is subtropical. Other parts of Russia need ice palaces – we don't.'

He was killed in the most awful way – near the Kremlin and under FSB cameras, so the recordings were never released and the investigation was a sham. But there was one grainy camera recording, taken from far away, which showed that two killers had methodically shot him from the front and behind. How symbolic it was!

Nemtsov's assassination was a turning point in my attitudes towards the past, and the future. I was unable to express what I was thinking, but I was becoming deeply troubled and despairing for the fate of my country. I couldn't help but see the parallel between Nemtsov's killing and our collective assassination of Olympic ideals at Sochi. In both cases the FSB had numerous cameras recording what actually happened. And in both cases, only lies and falsifications have ever surfaced.

More to the point, I realised that I had to look out for myself. While I was in Cologne attending another annual Manfred Donike Workshop, Dr Rabin called to inform me that I would be meeting with the Independent Commission's investigator Günter Younger the following day. We met in my favourite restaurant in Cologne, Kulinarius on Dürener Street. He showed up with a silent colleague and was quite aggressive. He didn't understand much about doping control and had no concept of what it meant to be responsible for the investigation of 25,000 urine and blood samples each year as a laboratory director.

At the end of our talk, Günter played his trump card: if I told the IC the whole story, he could arrange for my family to resettle in Europe.

'How will I live?' I asked.

'You will live on your savings,' Günter reassured me, 'and we will provide security.'

What he didn't realise was that most Russians had no savings. In fact, I was deeply in debt, being in the middle of building a new cabin on the plot of my family's dacha in the country. Before he died, my father had ordered me to take possession of the property and completely restore it, in anticipation of my grandchildren.

'I have no money,' I snapped, and that was the end of our conversation.

Rabin called me to ask what I thought of Günter. I replied that the conversation hadn't amounted to much because he knew less about the ins and outs of doping control than I had been led to expect. Rabin laughed and thanked me for my remarks.

That was in early March 2015. Three weeks later, I was back in Lausanne for a meeting with Rabin and Dick Pound, who was chairing the ongoing IC investigation. We met in a crepuscular private room in the basement of the Palace Hotel. Pound had settled into a huge armchair and grimaced when I entered the room. He made a little speech that made no sense at all and then Rabin interrogated me for three hours, stubbornly reviewing the list of concerns in his notebook. He hammered away at the same question: How was it that when dirty samples arrived in Moscow, they always emerged clean? I told him several times that I didn't know what he was talking about.

Every time I answered, Rabin glanced over at Pound to gauge his reaction, but Pound had long since nodded off. Now I understood how he had risen to the top of the international sports movement; though he looked fast asleep, he never snored or rolled his head to one side and appeared to be fully engaged.

The 'Canadian gang', our name for Pound and his deputy, the lawyer Richard McLaren, told us to expect them back in late June, but instead they sent a team of five investigators, including Günter Younger. When they came to my office in the ADC, they suggested that we talk at a restaurant, assuming that our premises were bugged.

We talked on the veranda of the Moon Courtyard café for three hours. Their first question threw me for a loop: how many Visa Gold credit cards did I have with the VTB Bank? I had never been to this bank and didn't have a single card from them. I was carrying two Citibank cards – a gold credit card and a salary debit card. Those were my only cards.

Then they asked me about Evgeny Blokhin, who they had heard frequented RUSADA and my laboratory. What did I know about him? I told them that some security people had hung around the laboratory during the Sochi Games. Blokhin may have been one of them, but those people did not report to me.

In April, Nagornykh told me that it had been decided that the 'plumbers brigade' was being disbanded. He gave us no reason. We would have to learn how to work without swapping – the only cheating tool at our disposal would be the substitution of urine at the collection site, but Nikita Kamaev was uncomfortable with the deepening corruption of his DCOs. There was also the risk of 'unwanted positives', when an athlete consumed supplements he or she knew nothing about. If this urine found its way into sealed A and B BEREG-kit bottles, I would have to report the AAF to ADAMS, or the ADC would lose its accreditation.

We had no choice and began our 'backwards perestroika'. In the summer of 2015, there were two major sporting events: the inaugural Olympics European Games in Baku in June, then the FINA World Swimming Championships in Kazan, a gorgeous, historic city on the Volga River. FINA's top anti-doping official, Cornel Marculescu, hadn't seen the ARD documentary so had no problem letting the Moscow Anti-Doping Centre handle all the doping control for the two-week-long event.

Mutko, anticipating the tsunami of criticism from the forthcoming WADA IC report, ordered us to play by the rules at Kazan: there was to be no collusion in sample collecting with RUSADA, no exchange of results and names, and all analyses would be downloaded to ADAMS immediately after completion. I said that I would obey the minister's directive, but wouldn't take responsibility for the consequences.

Here is what happens when you play by the rules: You lose.

Just before the swimming began, we received an out-of-competition positive result for ostarine, a substance that was often found in the urine of Russian athletes in tiny amounts. Ostarine positives made me furious – it generally came from inferior sports nutrition products – but I had no idea who was selling what to which athletes. After I cooled down, I asked Nagornykh whether it could be a Russian athlete? Perhaps I should ask Nikita Kamaev whose sample we were talking about?

Nagornykh kept silent for a minute and then remarked with a sarcastic smile: 'Dear Dr Rodchenkov, you are of course aware of the new position of our minister and his directives?'

In other words, new rules applied and RUSADA wouldn't be sharing sample data with us for useful purposes to protect athletes whose urine samples we found positive, or 'dirty'. I held my tongue and the ostarine was reported to ADAMS.

Then the tsunami hit: it turned out that the ostarine had been found in the urine of Yana Martynova, the 'Little Mermaid' of the championships. She had been born in Kazan, became world champion and had been chosen to recite the athletes' oath ('committing ourselves to a sport without doping and without drugs') at the opening ceremony that day. On live TV, broadcast all over the world, she stood next to Vladimir Putin and Mutko, while at the same moment in Moscow, I was in the process of downloading her adverse analytical finding to ADAMS.

It was a situation comparable only to the closing ceremony at Sochi, when Vladimir Putin stood next to the flag-bearer and champion bobsledder Alexander Zubkov inside the packed Fisht Olympic Stadium. We were in the nearby laboratory and could hear the music and cheers of the crowd, as we prepared to swap out his tainted urine sample and guarantee his second gold medal.

Mutko railed against the RUSADA top brass and demanded that we retract the positive result from ADAMS. I met Kamaev and Khabriev the next day, when they returned to Moscow. They looked like they were about to go to a funeral and begged me to do something. I reminded them of my Friday lecture from Nagornykh: I was just carrying out his orders.

That is Russian sporting history in a nutshell: a doped flag-bearer had led the national team into the Sochi Olympic Games and now another doper was endorsing sportsmanship and fair play, with President Putin standing next to his doped heroes.

In September, Blokhin came by my office to say goodbye – he was leaving for a new appointment in the FSB. I was going to miss him and his two assistants, our magicians Konstantin and Oleg, whose last names I never knew. I had no idea how we were going to protect our top athletes without him – after all, the 2016 Rio Olympics were just around the corner.

CHAPTER 7

THE BOMB EXPLODES

While we waited for Dick Pound's report to appear, I tried to get on with my life. In March, I had celebrated my tenth anniversary as director of the Moscow ADC, and in late October another anniversary rolled around: it was 30 years ago, on 30 October 1985, that I worked my first day as a junior researcher at the doping control laboratory in the VNIIFK institute, which the long-forgotten Dr. Vitaly Semenov converted to an independent enterprise in 1992, to weather the financial turbulence of *perestroika*.

I still had routine meetings with Nagornykh, where we discussed subjects like the upcoming 2016 Rio de Janeiro Olympics. But taking his cue from Mutko, he had suddenly become cautious. The Russians were under the microscope, and we certainly weren't drafting any ambitious swapping plans for Rio. We were like soldiers in a First World War trench, worried that an artillery shell from might land on our heads. And in early November, it did.

We heard the shell before we felt it. Nikita Kamaev had his ear to the ground and told me that the new IAAF president, Lord

Sebastian Coe, had met with Valentin Balakhnichev in Moscow. Nikita also heard that Lamine Diack, the former IAAF president, his lawyer Habib Cissé and Dr Gabriel Dollé, former director of doping affairs at the IAAF, had been arrested in Paris.

A harbinger of the IC report appeared on the IAAF website the day before its release. It seemed as if Coe had been tipped off that the report would condemn the IAAF's attitude toward sport doping and was covering his ass in the face of anticipated criticism:

Q: Can you confirm whether the information provided within that story [the ARD documentary] assisted in your own investigations into Russian athletics in any way, or even confirm that you ever investigated? If you did investigate, ahead of your flagship event [the 2013 IAAF World Championships in Moscow] what did you do, practically? If you didn't investigate, why not?

A: The claims centred on the WADA-accredited laboratory in Moscow, which was subsequently subject to a thorough investigation by WADA. You would have to ask WADA whether your article was useful for their investigations. Please be aware that the IAAF has no jurisdiction to investigate wrongdoing by WADA-accredited laboratories. As for the situation of doping in Russia, there can be no doubt, in light of the numerous high-profile athletes caught by the IAAF, that the IAAF has vigorously, and without any external help, chased Russian athletes suspected of doping. The list of sanctioned athletes caught by the IAAF speaks for itself.

It made me angry that Coe was taking credit for my work at the Anti-Doping Centre. It was my laboratory, with its state-of-the-art detection methodology for long-term metabolites of steroids, and new doping substances like peptides, ostarine and GW1516, that had caught these 'high-profile athletes'. Had the IAAF sent these samples to some other, mediocre, laboratory, they would have missed at least two-thirds of our AAFs and reported them as negative. Furthermore, if the IAAF 'caught' anyone using the athlete biological passport data, it was probably thanks to me. My Anti-Doping Centre had processed about three-quarters of all Russian blood data, in the form of over 20,000 blood analyses since 2010. I've never manipulated or tweaked blood data.

Coe was behaving like any politician would, jockeying for position and hoping not to be swept away by the tsunami of revelations that would emerge from Pound's IC report. His pre-varications were quickly forgotten when, on 9 November 2015, we got our first look at the report. I watched a live internet feed from Lausanne, while Dick Pound read the report page by page; within seconds, my secretary Anastasia was fighting off phone calls from newspapers and TV reporters around the world. *Life News* kept calling, and while trying to hang up on one of their pushy reporters, I inadvertently left the line open. So when I called Pound, McLaren and Younger the 'three dorks who understand nothing', *Life News* recorded it, and ten minutes later the audio clip went viral. It was not a great start.

The 323-page 'Report to the President of WADA of an Independent Investigation,' otherwise known as the 'Pound Report', exploded the Russian sporting world on 9 November. I've been critical of it, I've refuted many of its accusations and I've even made fun of it. But it changed my life forever.

In the harshest possible terms, the report condemned the 'systemic culture of doping in Russian Sport'. It identified many villains, but I was pretty much singled out as public enemy number one. In the executive summary, the report recommended closing the Moscow ADC 'and that its director be permanently removed from his position ... The IC further finds that the heart of the positive drug test cover-up is Director Rodchenkov.' I was also identified as 'an aider and abettor of the doping activities'.

The report rehashed the Stepanovs' allegations from Hajo's movie, and then added testimony from two 'confidential witnesses', whose identity I don't know to this day. They accused me of extorting money 'to execute the concealment [of] positive test results', which wasn't true. I was supposedly charging 50,000 roubles, or about $1,600, to cover up a positive result, but I had honestly never heard about this kind of thing until Pound's report. But the most shocking allegation was that the ARAF president Valentin Balakhnichev and I were operating shakedowns together; my share was apparently 20,000 roubles and Balakhnichev's was 30,000. This was absurd – I'd fallen out with Balakhnichev and hadn't spoken to him since 2010! I've never asked Balakhnichev for any favour, nor ever received any cent or rouble from him.

Pound's report also posited the existence of a 'second laboratory' in Moscow, which was something like the 'second shooter' of John F. Kennedy assassination conspiracy theory. It sounded suspicious, but they had simply mis-identified a laboratory that was used for younger athletes and lacked the expertise to pre-test any of the top athletes and experienced cheats.

They also dredged up the name of the notorious Russian steroid peddler Evgeny Evsukov, calling him 'a purported associate of Rodchenkov' and alleging that 'he has a contact at the Moscow laboratory'. This was nonsense – I'd met Evsukov a few times, but he'd never been near the entrance of my laboratory and all I knew about him was that he belonged in jail.

There was, however, plenty that the report got right. They reported on their many futile efforts to take samples at Chegin's race walking centre in Saransk, where doping 'shows no sign of stopping'. They were aware that FSB people were hanging around my laboratory, although they had no idea what they were doing. And they got the gist of the prevailing *bespredel* in Russian doping, even if their picture was a little fuzzy around the edges.

My first instinct, as always, was self-preservation. I had wrestled with WADA before, and knew I would have to defend the Anti-Doping Centre, our WADA accreditation and my 50 employees. I knew I could mount a serious defence before the Court of Arbitration for Sport, since each WADA sanction granted me 21 days to appeal. I wrote to Claude Ramoni, and he immediately confirmed that he would be happy to represent me. I felt better already.

The next day a letter arrived from Sir Craig Reedie: the Moscow ADC was suspended, all analyses should be terminated and we should stop downloading data to ADAMS. I rushed over to

Nagornykh's office, where I found the RUSADA boss Professor Khabriev and the ubiquitous, newly promoted Natalia Zhelanova. We needed to meet with Mutko, but he kept us waiting for an hour outside his office.

Mutko's spacious office had just been refurbished, doubtless to commemorate his recent appointment as chief of the powerful Russian Football Union. He was chatting about the latest gossip from the soccer world, as if the IC report was really such a big deal. Then he asked me what I was going to do, given that the ADC had had its accreditation suspended. I told him that he had 21 days to submit an appeal to CAS and that my lawyer Claude Ramoni was fired up and ready to go. I reminded Mutko that Ramoni had helped me beat WADA the last time they had tried to suspend the ADC, at Johannesburg in 2013.

The filmmaker Bryan Fogel got back in touch with me at around this time, partly to discuss his documentary and partly because he followed the news and was concerned about my welfare. He has a video of me confidently bragging that we 'will overturn this nonsense – it will be upside down.' But that wasn't going to happen. There would be no appeal to CAS and Ramoni would not be called into play. Instead it was going to be me who would be 'upside down.'

Mutko had made up his mind even before I walked into his office. He told me that I was thinking only about my own laboratory, and that I'd been operating on my own and violating all these anti-doping rules – a ridiculous suggestion, given his first-hand knowledge of our shenanigans! But he had decided not to pick a fight with WADA and concluded that it would be neither helpful nor productive to defend the ADC in front of CAS. He suggested I resign, but I later learned that he had received a letter from Craig Reedie, ordering my dismissal.

After pausing for a moment, he asked me who my successor should be. I said I could resign immediately, and that Dr Marina Dikunets should be appointed interim director. He agreed, and told me to make it happen.

I went straight to the human resources department and submitted my resignation letter, which terminated my contract with the Ministry of Sport. Then I grabbed Dikunets in the laboratory and took her to the Ministry, telling her as we walked that she had to sign the interim director contract. Mutko signed my contract termination and Marina was appointed interim director.

When we returned to the ADC, it felt as if the whole building were in mourning. My assistants were crying and some of the men in the office had started to drink. I filled a few cardboard boxes with the best books from my shelves and drove home.

The next day, television crews and reporters were buzzing around the Anti-Doping Centre. Natalia Zhelanova wanted to enter the laboratory, but I told security not to let her or anybody else in. A friend of mine with Kremlin connections suggested that I might need personal security for several days, and each time I drove to work I took a different route, accompanied by my bodyguard, who slept in my apartment and watched TV with my dog Vrangel, who kept watch, too.

On top of that, I learned from my remaining close friends that

Mutko had ordered them to keep an eye on me, to make sure that I didn't remove anything from the laboratory. But I had already backed up my office computer and removed the hard disc – there was nothing left to worry about.

In my diary for Friday, 13 November 2015, I noted an unproductive meeting with Yuri Nagornykh and Dr Dikunets. Nagornykh was trying to raise our spirits but I was desolate. Later that day another huge bomb exploded when the IAAF suspended ARAF for six months. That would have dire consequences: Russia would eventually be banned from participating in the 2016 Olympics in Rio de Janeiro and at the 2017 IAAF World Championships.

My telephone became useless because whenever I switched it on I was hit with an avalanche of calls from the media. I spent that Friday night at the gym, swimming, working out and relaxing in the sauna. As I drove home that night, I realised that all kinds of people had been calling Veronika, concerned about my well-being. I was at the centre of an international scandal pitting the Ministry of Sport against WADA and was a threat to them both. Friends who cared about my security told me that I should be careful while swimming – I might 'drown' or have a 'heart attack' in the sauna. I should avoid walking alone in the dark at night.

Then Hajo Seppelt called me out of the blue, with the same warning: 'You are in danger – don't spend time alone.' He and I had a complicated relationship: he valued me as a source, but also knew that his reporting had put me in danger. At one point, he had even offered to help me relocate my family to Germany. That seemed like a desperate idea at the time, but now? My friend in the Kremlin had warned me about my personal security and now suggested that my murder could be disguised as a suicide, supported by my prior attempt to take my own life.

I became paranoid, and could focus on only one thing: getting out of Russia. I knew I was being watched from all sides, so I'd have to conceal my intentions from everyone. I spent that weekend at home. Bryan Fogel had offered to come to Moscow to document my travails, footage that he could use for *Icarus*, but I told him that my situation was more urgent than that. We created new email addresses, adopted new Skype names and kept records of our conversations:

> Bryan: 'I'm worried about you.'
> GR: 'Me too. I'm in danger because I'm the only man who can kill both sides – Russia and WADA. I need to escape – but not officially.'
> Bryan: 'Would you come back, or just leave?'
> GR: 'I don't know, it depends. The situation is crazy.'

Bryan had a cruise planned with his family over Thanksgiving. He asked if this could wait a few days but I said no, that would be too late. He understood my position and sent me an electronic ticket for a return trip from Moscow to Los Angeles.

> Bryan: 'We'll make the ticket for two weeks. If you stay, you stay.'
> GR: 'Yes – better to leave, smile and keep your fingers crossed.'

Once I received that electronic ticket for Tuesday 17 November 2015, I felt happy, relaxed even, for the first time in days. Finally there was a flicker of light at the end of the tunnel.

Veronika had been monitoring my increasing desolation and asked what was going on. I told her that the cold November had taken a toll on me and that I'd decided to spend winter in balmy LA; after a break, we could plan our lives again, but I told her to keep that top-secret. She saw how exhausted I was and shared in my suffering. 'I cannot watch how you are suffering here, nervous and lost. It would be better for both of us if you left Moscow for a few months.'

Anna Chicherova, the 2012 Olympic high jump champion and poster girl of Russian athletics, called me on Saturday. She was desperate – because of the ARAF suspension, she wouldn't be going to Rio and her career was in ruins. I invited her to come and see me, and we walked on my favourite island in the middle of the rowing canal. My dog Vrangel's long red fur and tail were flying in the wind, in contrast to the gloomy weather. But despite the gloom, it was not end of my life – it was end of my life in Moscow.

Monday 16 November 2015 was the toughest day of my life. I went to work to sign some documents that had not been properly dealt with when I was director. Then I sat through a useless meeting with Nagornykh. He was tired and pessimistic but for some reason was trying to boost my spirits, which had the opposite effect. I became aloof and distant and felt as if my soul had already left Russia for Los Angeles. When I said goodbye to Nagornykh, I knew it was for the last time. I felt like a machine, devoid of emotions. When I had been ADC director, I loved to banter with my staff, and listen to their problems and needs. Stripped of my job, I didn't need to speak to anyone. And no one seemed eager to speak with me.

In my mind, I ticked off any threats that could possibly hinder my departure plan. I asked my IT expert to check my police account; there were still five summons for moderate speeding, each of 500 roubles. It wasn't much, but I was determined to destroy all possible obstacles, so I drove to the bank and paid the tickets.

It was my last time in the ADC and I sat behind my desk, but felt nothing. The next day I would have to slip away from my bodyguard and disorient anyone who might be following me. I loudly announced that my car was out of order and that the repair service would be coming tomorrow, establishing that I planned to spend the following day at the laboratory, in order to monitor the repairs. I stealthily registered for my flight for the next day and printed out a boarding pass.

Yuri Chizhov drove me home with my security guard, who I told was free to leave – Nagornykh had asked me to prepare a memo about the current doping scandals, so I would be better off working at home. Chizhov would spend the night at my apartment and would return me safely to the ADC tomorrow.

'That car is such a headache!' I kept repeating, reinforcing the idea that I would be at the ADC to supervise its repair. I knew my phone calls were being monitored and wanted to throw my minders off the scent. Then I called my son Vasily and asked him to come to see me early the next morning, to help his mother with her computer. I drank some whisky and slept soundly.

The next morning, Vasily came to breakfast and I served him sunny-side-up eggs, as usual. Vrangel was meowing like a cat – Pomeranians are very musical and emit a panoply of sounds when they smell freshly cooked food – and I gave him some snacks. As usual. Then I confided that we would be driving to Sheremetyevo International Airport because I was flying to LA to cure my asthma. Don't use your cell phone or tell anyone where we are going, I warned Vasily and Yuri. We would be taking two cars – if a traffic cop stopped one of them or it got a flat tyre, I would take the backup car. I then telephoned my accountants and told them I would be coming to the laboratory in a couple of hours.

At the airport, I gave Vasily my winter coat and hugged him and Yuri, before walking through border control and customs. I wasn't carrying any luggage because a baggage check might provide a pretext for keeping me off my flight. I had a small carry-on bag containing my Sochi laptop, the hard drive of my office computer, a couple of swimsuits and my running shoes – everything I'd need for a two-week stay in Los Angeles.

On board, I slept and ate and then slept again. Bryan and his cameraman greeted me on arrival at LAX and I watched the sun set in Los Angeles, my favourite American city! We rented a car, and in the darkness I carefully followed Bryan to my new home in central Los Angeles. It was 5am Moscow time and I fell into a deep sleep. My new life had begun.

PART IV

EXILE

CHAPTER 1

THE LOS ANGELES EARTHQUAKE

As soon as I'd conquered my jet lag and the anxiety associated with acclimating myself to such new surroundings, Bryan pressed me into service for his *Icarus* documentary. My role was to explain the chemistry of sport doping and the loopholes in doping control practice, and to help them understand which angles to pursue. A top-level amateur cyclist, Bryan wanted to prove that he could dramatically improve his time in the gruelling seven-day alpine race between Mègeve and Nice using undetectable doping strategies. I explained to him the fundamental rule of doping in sport: the important thing was not that the doping preparations he was taking were undetectable but *when* they were detectable. If the testing occurred at the right time and place, he might get caught.

Even though I was staying in a different part of town, Bryan was my host in LA, and we spent many hours getting to know each other. He was a talented journalist with good interviewing instincts. He filmed me numerous times, and I began to feel more expansive about sharing some of my doping secrets. No one was watching and the stakes seemed low, so I began to answer questions more freely.

For his part, Bryan kept pressing me harder and asking for more detail. He started calling me a 'shark', and then joked that he had landed 'a big fish'. 'You are the megashark,' he said to me one day. He was joking but also deadly serious. 'I know you are keeping something secret. A nuclear-sized secret.'

Bryan insisted on knowing what I was holding back. And of course, I had brought something to Los Angeles with me other than my laptop and running gear. Outside of Russia, I was the sole possessor of perhaps the greatest secret in twenty-first-century sport: I knew that the Russians had devised an unimaginably audacious cheating scheme for the Sochi Olympics, and got away with it.

I started thinking about Operation Sochi Resultat and how remarkable it had been. Tampering with the tamper-proof BEREG-kit bottles, opening the caps without damaging them and then swapping the pre-tested urine before passing it back through the nearly invisible 'mousehole'. It was a perfect operation, which we pulled off without a single mistake. It worked 'like a Swiss clock', as a confidential witness noted in the Pound Report.

Furthermore, we had left no trace – there were no remaining records, documents or digital footprints. I'd destroyed all my files and emails, and I constantly demanded that my staff immediately erase messages with sample numbers or scans of the doping control form.

Who else could tell this story? My assistants, Yuri Chizhov and Evgeny Kudryavtsev, couldn't communicate in English, and furthermore they didn't know the whole story. Evgeny Blokhin probably knew enough to explain what happened in Sochi, but why would he want to? He had moved on to a new assignment with the FSB and for all I knew was working under a new name by now.

If you started telling this story inside Russia, you might not make it home alive. Chizhov and Kudryavtsev both had families. In Russia, you could die during a staged fight after a minor road accident, when some guy pulled out a hammer and crushed your skull, or when some 'altercation' arose on the street.

Although I felt relaxed in Los Angeles, keeping the Sochi story bottled up left me on edge. I knew that telling the truth was hugely important, but also that the messenger would have a target on his back. I don't consider myself paranoid, but I am realistic. It was around this time that the long-awaited report on Alexander Litvinenko's 2006 poisoning in London was going to be released and there was plenty to fear. The FSB killers had many different ways of silencing 'enemies of the state' and poisoning those enemies had been part of a state-sponsored programme developed over decades.

Nonetheless, I realised that I had to talk. The simple thought hit me each day that if something were to happen to me, the Sochi story would never be told. Feeling paranoid, I made a copy of my Moscow office computer and Sochi laptop hard drives that contained 50,000 files and gave it to Bryan, asking him to keep it in a safe place. Unsurprisingly, that made him both nervous and suspicious.

'What's on that drive?' he asked me numerous times, his

journalist's antennae vibrating. I could tell he was wondering whether I had information that might affect the documentary he was shooting.

'What's on that drive is so complex that it would take me several days to explain,' I answered. But Bryan was relentless and wouldn't be dissuaded. Late one evening, I finally spat it out and told him that we had swapped samples in the Sochi laboratory. I don't think either of us fully understood the magnitude of what I had revealed. We agreed that I would answer all his questions on camera the following day and scheduled a three-hour interview for me to unburden myself for the first time.

On Tuesday 22 December, Bryan and his cameraman, Andrew Siegman, came to my apartment and set up four cameras for what would prove to be a historic shoot. We spent three hours recording what we would later call the 'black jacket' interview, because I'm wearing a dark ash-coloured Pierre Cardin fleece jacket throughout. It would be the first time I or anyone on the planet had spoken publicly about the Sochi cheating scheme.

Bryan: 'Does Russia have a systematic, state-wide doping system in place to cheat the Olympics?'
GR: 'Yes.'
Bryan: 'Were you the mastermind of the state-wide system that cheated the Olympics?'
GR: 'Of course.'

Everything came out: the bare-knuckle fight with WADA; the accreditation of the Sochi laboratory; the Olympic Games; the

FSB magicians tampering with the BEREG-kits; and the drama of the late-night swapping sessions. I felt relaxed to have relieved myself of the psychological burden.

When we had finished recording, we made several backup tapes and stored each one in a separate, secure place. That day, I wrote in my diary: 'It's over. Now I can sleep quietly. Nothing will be lost. Manuscripts don't burn.' This last phrase was from Mikhail Bulgakov's classic novel, *The Master and Margarita*.

Did I feel myself transformed into a truth-teller, a whistle-blower or a traitor to my country? To be honest, I did not. I was simply pleased to see how Bryan became progressively more amazed as I told my story.

I also had problems that weighed more heavily on me than what happened at Sochi. My US visa was about to expire, I was running out of asthma inhalers, had no idea how I was going to finance my dacha construction project back in Russia and missed my family terribly.

*

I didn't completely understand what had just happened, but Bryan did. He was no longer making a documentary about Lance Armstrong and doping in the world of elite cycling and was instead making a movie about the greatest sports scandal of the twenty-first century: Russia's unprecedented commitment to cheating in international competitions.

A key story element was the FSB's brilliant reverse engineering of the BEREG-kit bottles. It was a miracle that I would never have believed possible until I saw it with my own eyes. Bryan needed some bottles so he could explain on film how they had been opened and swapped in the Sochi laboratory. I called Nikita Kamaev in Moscow and asked him to send me a couple of BEREG-kits. He was not happy with that and started quoting WADA rules, pointing out that it would be suspicious if BEREG-kits with traceable Russian serial numbers appeared in Los Angeles.

'Cool down and send me some BEREG-kits,' I replied. 'Nothing seems out of place here – it's the home of the "Terminator"! Everybody's at home in Los Angeles!'

'OK,' Nikita eventually agreed, 'but you need to help me too. I've started to write a book about sports pharmacological programmes in the Soviet Union and Russia and would like your advice.'

'Pharmacology' was the widely used euphemism for doping. I was surprised and upset. 'Do you know how dangerous is to write such a book in Russia?' I exclaimed. 'Have you told anyone that you are writing it? One night your house will go up in smoke, with you and your computer inside!'

'Oh, *Grinya*, you are emotional, even paranoid and you always exaggerate your fears,' Nikita replied. 'I'll send you the BEREG-kits tomorrow. Relax'.

2016 promised to be a turbulent and exciting year, to put it mildly. Bryan and his producers began to worry about my security, and I moved to a safer location in Santa Monica. I started jogging again and built up my strength for writing, which proceeded slowly because I had to re-read and rewrite every chapter several times. My English is strong, but more suited to laboratories and conferences than the emotional retelling of my life story.

On 21 January, the British government published a report concluding that Russian agents were 'probably responsible' for the assassination of former FSB agent Alexander Litvinenko in London in 2006. Then Sports Minister Vitaly Mutko decided to take notice of my absence, mentioning in a press interview that Dr Tim Sobolevsky and I were both working in laboratories in Los Angeles. 'What's going on?' he asked. This was a bizarre thing to say, and only half-true. Tim had left Russia for his dream job at UCLA's Olympic Analytical Laboratory, but I was still supposedly in Southern California to alleviate my asthma.

Just a few days later, Vyacheslav Sinev, who ran RUSADA between its creation in 2008 and 2011, suddenly died. I phoned Nikita, who had succeeded Sinev in 2011, though he had lost that job two months previously – after the release of the Pound Report, WADA declared RUSADA to be non-compliant with the Code, and a month later Nikita and his patron, Professor Ramil Khabriev, were forced to resign.

We talked about our books and Nikita informed me that he had already contacted foreign publishers about his investigation into the history of doping since the Soviet era.

'Do you have any idea what you're doing?' I exclaimed. 'You will infuriate so many people, you will have so many new enemies, you cannot even imagine! Look, you have an apartment in Valencia, so go there and write – don't do it in Russia! And please, make several copies of your book and documents, and store them among reliable friends. And make complete backups each week – your computer might be hacked.'

As usual, Nikita pushed back against my tirade. 'There are no computer files – I'm writing with pen on paper. I want to thank you again for your lovely fiftieth birthday present, this beautiful Montblanc pen. I'm writing my book in longhand – just like Balzac!'

'But why are you doing it in Russia?' I said again.

'Calm down – I've only jotted down about fifty pages of notes. No one could possibly perceive that to be a threat,' argued Nikita.

'In that case, please take pictures or scans of all your pages, for your own security and for backups!' I yelled.

But Nikita had no intention of taking my advice, or of leaving his home at the Ozero Krugloye resort ten miles outside Moscow, where he lived with his 85-year-old mother. He planned to spend the rest of the winter at home with her, working on his book. And he had no intention of making any copies – unlike me, he was not a paranoid alarmist and thought he was living in a normal country.

A few days later, on 14 February, I was working on my manuscript when I received a text message from Nikita's number: Гриша, Никита умер (Grisha, Nikita has died). I immediately called back, and his wife Anna answered. We wept and talked for over an hour.

'Do you know where his book is?' I asked Anna.

She didn't know what I was talking about.

'OK, maybe not a book, but where are the handwritten pages that he's been working on for the past few months?'

'I can't lay my hands on them,' she said, explaining that Nikita's mother had immediately locked his study and kept hold of the key. 'I can't confront her now, obviously . . .'

Nikita in Nyon, Switzerland, for a meeting at the UEFA
Headquarters in September 2015, six months before his sudden death.

I heard some noise in the background – the police had arrived
to confirm Nikita's death and draft their official report – and then
Anna's cell phone went dead. When I tried Nikita's, it wasn't
working either.

Just the day before, Nikita had been in high spirits. He had
even sent me a silly video of him fumbling with the motor of his
little snowmobile, trying to clean out some mechanical problem
with a twig.

On the day he died, Nikita visited his lawyer and then went
skiing in the forest next to his house. When he returned, he said
he felt weak. He lay down and realised almost immediately that
he was dying. He remarked to Anna what a banal ending it
seemed, and that he loved her very much. Within an hour, he was
dead in her arms.

To call his death a mystery would be an understatement.

Nikita never complained of heart problems, he never smoked and hardly ever drank alcohol. He was basically a workaholic and was either at his desk, or driving to and from work. He and I were colleagues at the VNIIFK back in the late 1980s, and often exercised together in the gym after work. We lived near the same forest and worked out together – I ran while he skied, and he'd curse me for damaging his trail with my footprints!

I was stunned and paralysed for a whole week, and then we received our final gift from Nikita – the two boxes of BEREG-kits we'd asked him for. How sad, and how ironic. We put them to excellent use in *Icarus*.

The Ministry of Sport completely ignored his funeral, sending neither a representative nor a wreath. To borrow a term from George Orwell's *1984*, Nikita had become an 'unperson'. Only Dr Avak Abalyan, a Ministry apparatchik who would lose his job to the doping scandal a few months later, came to the cemetery, on his own. I can imagine that Avak, a chronic chain smoker, had a few cigarettes at Nikita's gravesite.

When Nikita left RUSADA, he had, according to Vladimir Ivanov, the track and field correspondent for *Sport-Express*, received a particularly stark telephone message: 'It would be nice if you were dead. They would hang everything on you, and there would be no problems.'

When they brought Nikita's body to the Moscow regional forensic examiner, the autopsy was over in a flash. It was as if they had found a homeless drunk dead in the snow; they couldn't care less what had killed Nikita. There was a cursory inquest, and then the expected conclusion: he'd had a massive heart attack.

This was death by 'invisible inoculation', a familiar FSB practice. They wanted to bury him as soon as possible.

Nikita's death was a clear message to me. Given that the FSB had tapped his phone, they now knew that I was writing an expose of Russian doping. Two months had passed since the 'black jacket' interview, so they were probably aware that the state-sponsored Sochi swapping scheme wasn't going to stay secret for long.

By this time, I knew I had passed the point of no return. If I travelled home to Moscow, I would be locked in a psychiatric hospital until the day I died. The FSB would brand me a fabulist and would insist that my diaries were faked. In the end, that's exactly what they did, but no one believed them.

CHAPTER 2

GOING PUBLIC

In early 2016, I had renewed contact with an old acquaintance. It was slowly dawning on me that I was almost certainly going to become a Russian in exile, so I decided to reach out to someone who was in an almost exactly parallel situation: the main source for Hajo Seppelt's earth-shattering ARD documentary, Vitaly Stepanov.

I remembered the cherubic-faced Vitaly from Moscow, many years before. He had worked as a doping control officer for RUSADA, and because he spoke fluent English had also served as a valuable interpreter. I remember meeting him once on a cold winter morning when he brought me some athletes' samples. We had never spoken before, but I noticed his haggard appearance and his expensive but severely worn running shoes.

'Are you in training?' I asked. He told me he was preparing for the Boston Marathon in April, so had flown his samples to Moscow at four in the morning, run 15 kilometres and then brought the samples to the ADC.

I was amazed, and told him so. 'How can you do serious

training after a sleepless night! You're torturing your body!' I lost track of him after that, until he and his wife Yuliya emerged as the stars of Hajo's film. His whistle-blowing formed the core of the Pound Report, which led directly to my dismissal and escape to the US.

So why had I struck up a relationship with him on Skype? As I mentioned, we were both Russians living in exile in America, and even though his wife had broadcast some fantasies and gossip about me, I didn't blame Vitaly. He and I had plenty to talk about, including Yuliya's attempted comeback in the 800 metres, about which I was (correctly) quite sceptical. We knew the same people at RUSADA and the IAAF and talked about Nikita's death, about Hajo and Sinev. We discussed cooking, a hobby that I take very seriously. And inevitably, we also talked about the Olympic Games in Vancouver and Sochi.

Vitaly kept circling back to Sochi. How could it happen, he asked, that we performed so poorly at Vancouver and so superbly at Sochi, just four years later? Could that be done without any manipulation?

'You keep asking that,' I answered, 'but can't you figure it out? How could we fail to exploit such a favourable situation – an Olympic Games on Russian soil, with our own Olympic laboratory under my direction?'

Vitaly became visibly excited when I mentioned the names of five gold medal winners who had been on the doping programme. 'We helped them as much as we could,' I explained.

In six or seven separate conversations, we spoke for almost 15 hours. I didn't realise it, but Vitaly recorded every session – in retrospect, I accept that I had been a little naïve about my new 'friend'.

*

In the spring of 2016, Dan Cogan, one of the producers of *Icarus*, suggested something that hadn't occurred to us. We had evidence of a Sochi cheating scheme so brazen that it would almost certainly get the perpetrators kicked out of the Olympic Movement. Shouldn't we go public with this information before the Rio de Janeiro Summer Olympic Games, which were scheduled to open in August? The documentary wouldn't be finished by then, but he argued that we had a 'moral suasion' to inform the world about what had happened at Sochi before Rio.

We were warming to Cogan's idea, when the decision was made for us: in the middle of the night on 10 March, two FBI agents knocked on my door, ascertained that they had tracked down Grigory Rodchenkov and served me with a federal subpoena. I was to appear before a grand jury in New York City to testify in a case filed by the US Attorney for the Department of Justice.

These were the same prosecutors who had exposed endemic corruption in FIFA, the governing body of world soccer, and now they were coming after the self-styled lords of the world's anti-doping charade. The United States had been paying WADA several million dollars of taxpayers' money each year, but WADA's ability to enforce its own anti-doping rules now seemed 'illusory', to use the word uttered by Richard McLaren when Bryan had interviewed him earlier in the year. By way of representing the

American taxpayer, the Department of Justice had come after me, the famous 'aider and abettor' of the doping outrages.

For the moment, they had summoned me as a 'cooperating witness', which was good news; I was not, for the moment, the target of an investigation or an indictment. If I told them every-thing, my lawyer explained, I would probably avoid jail.

However, as a cooperating witness, I could not make any pub-lic statements about matters that were under investigation, which meant I could not discuss the Sochi cheating before the Rio Olympics. The Russians would hoover up all the medals they could in Brazil, doping or no doping.

We decided to take a big risk. First, we would go public with our Sochi revelations – the FSB involvement, the use of the 'cocktail', the massive bank of 'clean' samples and the secret swapping – and then I would present myself for questioning. The Department of Justice investigators might be *royally* ticked off that we had controlled the release of information they were seek-ing for themselves, but we had bought into Dan Cogan's 'moral suasion' argument. To broadcast our story, we planned to approach either CNN or the *New York Times*.

We flew to Atlanta to meet with CNN's top executives, but sensed that things didn't look good. We thought we were offering them a gold mine, but they didn't seem to agree. Their 'concerns' became clear a week or two later, when CNN announced that Media Alliance, 80 per cent of which was owned by Russia's National Media Group, had purchased the assets of Turner Broadcasting, which included CNN in Russia. The chair of the National Media Group board was Alina Kabaeva, the former gymnast who was rumoured to be the mother of Putin's children. As we say in Russia, 'Vsyo Yasno' – 'It's all clear.'

By contrast, the *New York Times* was very interested, and we were flattered by the attention of the most powerful and credible newspaper in the world. However, the organisation of all my information was going to be a problem. I had tons of unstructured data on computer hard drives and various email servers and while I could find my way through these jungles of information, it was simply too dense for newspaper journalists. The problem was how to translate my knowledge into language the average sport lover could understand. Even Bryan Fogel and his producer Andrew Siegman, who had been working with me for months, had trouble reconstructing the whole picture of the Sochi trickery, such was the complexity of the fraud.

So the three of us created a 100-page 'dossier' to explain the scandal to the *Times*. Its point of entry was a colourful PowerPoint presentation, with photographs and flow charts, convincingly describing the Sochi cheating scheme. Because in my words it looked unthinkable and impossible!

There was no aspect of my role in Russia's state-sponsored doping programme that we refused to discuss, and one of our assertions would soon be repeated around the world: 'This was a fraud of unspeakable proportion. It undermines all accomplishments and the whole system of doping control in sports.'

Two *New York Times* reporters, Rebecca Ruiz and Michael Schwirtz, spent three days with us in Los Angeles in early May. Rebecca had been covering the international doping story, while Michael had worked as a correspondent in Moscow and understood how Russia worked. I knew my story seemed incredible, so we invited my former colleagues Tim Sobolevsky and Oleg Migachev, creators of our Laboratory Information Management System (LIMS), to take a break from their jobs at the UCLA doping control laboratory and join us for part of a day.[10] Tim hadn't known about the night-time swapping because it was a secret FSB operation, but he did notice the constant presence of Yuri Chizhov and the 'plumber' Blokhin, even though the Sochi laboratory had no water supply problems.

Most importantly, Tim was able to confirm the ongoing analysis of urine samples from plastic containers in the Anti-Doping Centre and the creation of a so-called 'clean urine bank' at the CSP in Moscow. He knew that our LIMS had thousands of undisclosed results, either from unofficial, under-the-table research or from official, in- and out-of-competition analysis. All the tricks that we used to protect our cheats – what McLaren sardonically called our 'disappearing positive methodology' – were traceable in the LIMS.

After three days of intense questioning and discussion, Rebecca and Michael believed my story, but life can be full of surprises. On 5 May, in the middle of our interviews, the flagship CBS TV show *60 Minutes* boasted an enormous scoop: Russian athletes had doped during the Sochi Olympic Games. Their star witness was my 'friend', Vitaly Stepanov. Not only was he offering

10 The LIMS, which three years later would become the subject of international intrigue, was our proprietary database for the Moscow and Sochi laboratories.

his own, second-hand account of what happened in Sochi, but he had given *60 Minutes* excerpts of me talking about the five doped gold medallists, taken from our Skype conversations. The episode would be broadcast on Sunday 8 May, with a potential audience in the tens of millions.

We were deeply upset. I tried to reconstruct what I had told Vitaly during our 15 hours of Skyping, and to imagine what he could stitch together from my comments. On the one hand we wanted the truth to be known for the sake of history, but my life was also at stake and the information I possessed was my one bargaining chip with the US government. Vitaly revealing everything before I'd had a chance to speak would be a nightmare.

Suppose the *New York Times* walked away from their project, angry that what we had insisted were exclusive revelations had become yesterday's news? We had to defend our story. Vitaly had no right to record my comments and publish them without my approval, so my lawyers promptly notified him and CBS to that effect.

In the end, our worries were somewhat misplaced; when *60 Minutes* aired, it was little more than a carbon copy of Hajo's documentary that had been broadcast in Europe 18 months previously, though Vitaly's rosy cheeks and perfect English made everything he said seem completely believable.

To be fair, they did have had something new to offer: me. 'Another exile in the US for the same reason is Grigory Rodchenkov, who ran Russia's drug testing lab,' a voiceover intoned. 'No one knows more about doping in Russia than Rodchenkov, who says he could make positive test results disappear.'

According to the documentary, I had told Stepanov that FSB agents helped Russia cheat at the 2014 Winter Olympics in Sochi. He also claimed that I'd told him I had the 'Sochi List' of Russians who competed on steroids, four of whom were gold medal winners. What Vitaly called the 'Sochi List' was the famous 'Duchess List'.

In the end, the *60 Minutes* film functioned as little more than a teaser for the *New York Times* story, a flare sent up into the dark sky before we unleashed our artillery barrage on the Olympic Movement. We had a much bigger story to tell.

The *Times* article appeared on its website around noon on 12 May. Bryan set up cameras in my apartment to record me reading and reacting to the story online in real time. The 3,000-word account had an immense impact. It explained who I was and what I had done, as well as every detail of the swapping operation. It also included a separate explanation, with illustrations, of how the scheme was carried out. They even used the photograph of the 'mousehole' that I had taken on my last day in Sochi, when Yuri Chizhov and I were saying goodbye to our beloved laboratory. The article also named names, among them the 'three Alexanders': the gold medal dopers Zubkov, Legkov and Tretyakov. Rebecca and Michael had done a fantastic job.

The next day we scrambled to find a copy of the print edition, but by the time I started looking, all the coffee shops in LA's Westside had sold out. Andrew and I finally found it on sale in a petrol station in Santa Monica; we bought several copies and revelled in our collective work.

It would be impossible to overstate the impact of what we had done. In late 2014, Hajo had told the world that the Russians had been doping for several consecutive Olympics, but his mouthpieces were generally outsiders, many of them former dopers who harboured resentments for being excluded from the plush training camps and 'pharmacology' programmes reserved for the select few. The principal players – Balakhnichev, Portugalov, Mutko, Nagornykh, Kamaev, Zhelanova and myself – naturally kept our traps shut. And when Dick Pound followed up on Hajo's work, the Russian sports machine stonewalled him.

But I was the main actor in the Sochi scandal, and I had a veritable mountain of evidence backing me up, including the photos and the doctored spreadsheets rescued from my hard drive at the ADC. It's true that I had deleted plenty of evidence, but I had more than enough material to expose the inner workings of Russia's sports fraud.

WADA hastily assembled a second investigation, this one conducted by a so-called 'independent person', Richard McLaren, the Canadian lawyer who had worked with Dick Pound on the first independent commission. McLaren had only one job: to determine whether or not I was telling the truth.

McLaren wasn't able to come to Los Angeles on 20 May because he was in Paris, so we connected on Skype. Top-level representatives of WADA and the IOC decided to participate, and came to LA. Bryan organised a press conference for them, using some of the presentation materials we had prepared for the *New York Times*. When they started perusing the dossier we had assembled, they expressed shock. And then Bryan broke the silence: 'There was no doping control in Russia. Not at all. Never.'

After Bryan gave a presentation, each attendee received a folder filled with documents and photos. I attended via Skype, and watched the reaction on each attendee's face, as their hope that the *New York Times* had got the story wrong abandoned them. It was true: Russia had perpetrated an epochal doping fraud, right under their noses.

I was unable to attend the meeting because my security situation had changed, and not for the better – outraged Russian athletes and sports bureaucrats were issuing veiled and not-so-veiled death threats against me. I had to move out of my funky Santa Monica cabin to a more secure residence with an underground car park, which made it harder to track my comings and goings. I also changed cars and licence plates.

From the late spring of 2016 until the present day, 'normal life' has been a luxury I am unable to enjoy.

CHAPTER 3

WELCOME TO 'UNPERSONHOOD'

'Opening the kimono' on the secrets from Sochi was the right thing to do. The sports world was well on its way to plumbing the depths of the gargantuan Russian doping operation, but the revelations created problems for me as well for Russian sport.

As predicted, the story in the *New York Times* angered the Department of Justice prosecutors at the Eastern District of New York. They didn't answer my lawyer's calls for several days, and we began to worry that the next document I received would be an indictment, which would bring with it the threat of jail. Luckily, Bryan and his associates found me the perfect criminal defence lawyer. Jim Walden specialised in protecting defendants *in extremis*. He had worked in the Department of Justice, and in every case he had accepted as a private lawyer, he had managed to successfully change his client's status from accused criminal to cooperating witness. He did have some doubts about me: sport wasn't his field, and the intricacies of my alleged crimes were dauntingly complex.

We agreed to meet in Philadelphia, where we talked and signed a contract. If I made any public statements from then on, they would come from Walden. He and his colleague Avni Patel also helped me prepare for interrogation by Department of Justice investigators, and vetted any information I supplied to McLaren and his associates.

By the middle of the year, I had left Los Angeles, assumed a new identity and had to learn to respond to a new name.

In mid-June 2016, the bombs began to drop. The IAAF Council decided to extend the disqualification of Russian track and field athletes from international competitions, meaning that they would be barred from the Rio Olympic Games in July. The IOC stated that neither Sports Minister Mutko nor any of his employees would be accredited in Rio, and the IOC and the Court of Arbitration for Sport (CAS) in Lausanne upheld the IAAF's decision. Then yet another bomb landed: the IPC had disqualified the entire Russian Paralympic team! We were in a state of disbelief.

On 18 July, just two weeks before the start of the Rio Games, McLaren released his report, in which every statement I had made was vindicated. McLaren concluded 'beyond reasonable doubt' that Russia's Ministry of Sport, the Centre for the Sports Preparation of the National Teams of Russia (the CSP), the FSB and the ADC had 'operated for the protection of doped Russian athletes' within a 'state-directed failsafe system' using 'the disappearing positive methodology'.

Of course, each new report provoked a new round of frantic ass-covering. The Switzerland-based Berlinger Group, manufacturers of the BEREG-kit bottles, stated emphatically that they still regarded their product as tamper-proof: 'We have no knowledge of the specifications, the methods or the procedures involved in the tests and experiments conducted by the McLaren Commission.'

Since May, Russia had been mobilising its own propaganda resources. Mutko acted as if the dramatic revelations had nothing to do with him. In an hour-long interview with Hajo Seppelt, he recited nonsense and avoided giving answers to direct questions. Then Vladimir Pozner, a Russian TV correspondent, put Mutko on the spot: who was lying about the swapping at Sochi – him or me? Instead of answering the question, Mutko blurted out some vague prevarication, causing Posner to take pity on him and back off. Mutko was one of the odd characters of the Putin era – colourful, with a combination of elegance and negligence. When pressed, he reverted effortlessly to the rote phrases of the veteran bureaucrat. He had limited talent or power, but he knew whom to hide behind: Vladimir Putin, a man with equally little talent, but considerable power.

On 18 June 2016, the Investigation Committee of Russia opened a criminal case against me, accusing me of abuse of authority, operating illegal businesses, forging documents and causing reputational damage to the country and its sports teams. On Russian websites, people started recalling the murder in exile of Leon Trotsky, by an assassin armed with an ice pick, speculating that I would not be allowed to remain alive for long.

Once again, I bought a new cell phone, changed my number and moved to a new safe house.

The Kremlin was calling me a defector and a traitor, but where was my homeland? Putin's Russia is a disgrace to the whole world – my real homeland was the forest and meadows between Romashkovo and Razdory on the western edge of Moscow, where I have been running all my life.

In Moscow, my favourite places were the Olympic venues, the 8.5-mile Olympic cycling circuit and the rowing canal, where I walked my dog Vrangel, not far from my home in Krylatskoye.

I had become an 'unperson', like Nikita Kamaev, except I was still alive. I knew I would never go home again.

*

It felt extraordinary to greet the new year of 2017 by watching not *The Irony of Fate*, the Soviet-era romantic comedy that plays on Russian television every 31 December, but *Pretty Woman*, a completely different sort of romantic fare. But the effect was the same. I was drinking wine and had tears in my eyes.

During the winter I often felt melancholy and desperately lonely. I was safe, but that meant cutting off contact with other human beings. 'No eye contact and maintain an aloof appearance,' were my instructions for when I left my apartment. I couldn't shop for groceries at my local supermarket or hunt for bargains at the mall. I also spent time talking to myself and to the television set.

From the moment I broke my silence about the Sochi swapping scheme, I had been the target not only of credible death threats but also of a relentless campaign of vilification emanating from Russia. Every fact of mine that had been confirmed by Dick Pound and Richard McLaren was denounced as fiction by the Russian authorities.

The Investigation Committee of Russia issued a series of threatening denunciations. The so-called 'Sochi cocktail' didn't exist, they insisted. They 'confirmed' this by interviewing 700 athletes, coaches, medical workers of the Russian national teams, employees of CSP and beneficiaries of the national sports federations, and not one of them had ever heard about a doping programme. 'If there were any anti-doping rule violations, they were purely individual in nature,' the committee concluded. FSB involvement was never mentioned nor even hinted at.

The ICR argued that no one could have broken into the BEREG-kit bottles: 'McLaren's argument about the possibility of opening the . . . bottles for storing doping samples of athletes manufactured by the Swiss company Berlinger is invalid and refuted,' they concluded, quoting 'experts' who 'gave an opinion on the impossibility of opening a completely closed bottle cap without destroying its integrity'.

They decided that I had concocted my accusations while under the influence of psychotropic drugs, and at the behest of the American 'special services', by which they meant the CIA.

The 'investigation' was just the tip of the iceberg. The notorious Basmanny District Court, which had targeted me back in 2011, issued a warrant for my arrest; they wanted to have me extradited from US soil. The Ministry of Sport declared that it would seek compensation for the damage I had done to Russian sport, and the authorities decided to seize my dacha, which I had inherited from my grandparents. Fortunately, Russian law prevented them from seizing the apartment where my family was still living.

All this was just preparing the ground for a step that would have lasting consequences. Thirty-nine of the athletes who had been disqualified for life, stripped of their medals and banned by the IOC from the forthcoming 2018 Winter Olympics in Pyeongchang, South Korea, appealed the decision of the Olympic Committee in Arbitration in Sport (CAS). The huge crowd of athletes and their entourage was too big for the Lausanne venue, so the hearings were moved to Geneva. This came close to achieving one of the Russian government's aims, which was for me to testify in a court of law, but my lawyers arranged that I could provide testimony via teleconference; I wouldn't have to go to Switzerland.

I testified on 22 January 2018. The cross-examinations were tricky, because it required multiple translation from English to Russian and back again and although I knew both languages, I would be facing people who would be anxious to point out the smallest contradictions in my testimony. I had an excellent translator by my side, but there was still every reason to be vigilant.

We managed to secure a stable video conference link from our hotel in New York, but on the Swiss side, Skype was hiccupping. Sometimes it was so hard to hear that questions had to be repeated, broadcast through someone's cell phone. Alexander Legkov, one of the 'three Alexanders', was the lead plaintiff for the disqualified Russians, the IOC having stripped him of his gold and silver medals in cross-country skiing from Sochi.

This proved to be a no-holds-barred legal dogfight, gravely inconvenienced by the poor communications with Lausanne. Legkov's lawyer asked me if I had personally seen the athletes donate clean urine, ingest the cocktail or forward scans of their doping control forms. I said no – other people did that.

When I asked for a few minutes to explain how the cocktail worked, I was turned down. This was reported in the Russian press as me asking for extra time to recall the ingredients of my cocktail! When I confirmed that I hadn't made the cocktail for the athletes on the 'Duchess list', and never saw the athletes use the cocktail, witnessed the collection of the athletes' clean urine before the Games or received the scans of doping control forms from the athletes, the Russian press concluded that I denied my previous testimony!

The issue of FSB involvement never arose, because CAS had agreed beforehand that each case would be considered individually and without reference to any alleged state-run programme or FSB involvement.

In the end, the CAS judges noted that it was very likely that during the Sochi Games some Russian athletes might have been involved in sample swapping, but that was not the case before them. They had been asked to determine the individual guilt or innocence of each petitioning athlete and could not 'comfortably satisfy themselves' that Alexander Legkov deserved to be stripped of his Olympic gold and silver medals on the basis of the evidence they had heard.

CAS upheld the appeal filed by Legkov[11] and 27 other athletes against the decision of the IOC, which meant that their results

11 CAS 2017/A/5379 Alexander Legkov v. International Olympic Committee (IOC).

and their medals earned in Sochi were reinstated. However, the IOC – infuriated by this decision – would not allow them to compete at the Pyeongchang Games, which were due to start a week later.

Another one of the 'Alexanders', the bobsled medallist and Sochi flag-bearer Zubkov,[12] wasn't as lucky as Legkov. CAS maintained the decision made by the IOC to strip him of his two Sochi golds[13] and wouldn't allow him to appear in South Korea. I remember that after his triumph at Sochi, Zubkov had presented Irina Rodionova with a diamond necklace and earrings. Irina then spent a week asking me how to divide the gifts. The tenth time she raised the subject, I told her to keep the gift and that I didn't need anything from Zubkov. For me, the best gift now is that his career is over.

In the end, 168 nominally neutral Russian athletes competed at the Pyeongchang Olympics, but not under the Russian flag. Three days after the Games, the IOC reinstated the Russian Olympic Committee and six months later, WADA reinstated RUSADA. The pendulum was swinging, and not in a good way.

12 CAS 2017/A/5422 Aleksandr Zubkov v. International Olympic Committee (IOC).

13 In separate adjudications, the IOC and the International Biathlon Union stripped three other Russian athletes of Sochi medals.

CHAPTER 4

SHELTER FROM THE STORM

I remember 4 March 2018 as a magical day. I was in a New York hotel room with two security guards, when the actor Laura Dern

Bryan Fogel with the Academy Award for *Icarus*.

and the director Greta Gerwig walked onto the stage of the Dolby Theatre in Los Angeles to announce the Academy Award for Best Documentary. Well before they started fumbling with the envelope, I blurted out '*Icarus*'. And *Icarus* it was.

Bryan took the stage and made a brief but emotional speech. I won't ever forget his final remarks: 'We dedicate this award to Dr Grigory Rodchenkov, a fearless whistle-blower who now lives in grave danger. We hope *Icarus* is a wake-up call, yes about Russia, but about more than that – about the importance of telling the truth.'

George Orwell would have been proud, and so was I.

*

That Oscar night felt like a precious dream wrapped inside a never-ending nightmare. Russia was waging a non-stop campaign of vilification and threats against me. Vitaly Mutko appealed his lifetime ban from the Olympic Games, alleging in his presentations that Nikita Kamaev, Tim Sobolevsky and I were running a criminal extortion ring and threatening to report athletes' samples positive if they didn't pay us. This was complete nonsense, not least because Nikita and Tim didn't know each other and had never communicated in their lives. But if you can't argue the facts, attack the messengers: Tim and I were conveniently out of reach in the United States and Nikita was conveniently dead.

Mutko convinced Chizhov and Kudryavtsev to testify that there had never been a 'mousehole' for sample swapping and they insisted that if there had been, WADA inspectors would have discovered it. In fact, Chizhov drilled the hole in October 2013, and there were not any inspections afterwards. It is true that Thierry Boghosian visited the laboratory in November 2013 and Olivier Rabin came in January 2014, but they never entered Rooms 124 and 125. Even if they had, to find the hole they would have had to move furniture and filing cabinets, which was not in their WADA job description.

Mutko had nothing to say about Irina Rodionova, Evgeny Blokhin or the 'plumbers' from the FSB. According to him, he hardly ever saw me, but I kept a log of our meetings between 2008 and 2015: we had 46 private meetings and 41 general events where I was present with athletes, coaches and Ministry employees.

I don't know what the CAS arbiters made of all this, but they

Evgeny Kudryavtsev, who denied the mousehole had ever existed. If you look at the bottom right corner, the floor and walls are the same as the mousehole photo on page 189.

set aside his lifetime Olympic ban on a technicality. They refused to address the question of Mutko's complicity in the sample swapping at Sochi, asserting that the IOC had no power over him because he was neither an athlete, a coach nor an official member of the Russian delegation to the Sochi Games. Meanwhile, Mutko had been luxuriating in his office inside the building of the Organising Committee for 'Sochi 2014' and palling around with his protector Putin.

Now Mutko was free to claim that Russia had 'cleaned up its mess', and, just like Alexander Legkov and the others, he had the 'exoneration' of the Court of Arbitration for Sport to prove it.

Emboldened by the CAS decisions in Switzerland, the billionaire oligarch and biathlon promoter Mikhail Prokhorov underwrote a defamation lawsuit filed against me in New York in 2018, on behalf of some Russian athletes. 'I am prepared to hire the best lawyers to defend the interests of our biathletes in any country of the world, where it will be most appropriate,' he told TASS, the Russian state news agency.

The litigants are hoping to use the American legal system to intimidate me. Having said that, to prove defamation in the United States, you need to establish both the falsehood of the allegation and 'actual malice', meaning that I accused people of doping when I knew for a fact that they did not. But I have never done that.

We countersued Prokhorov, and my lawyers and I look forward to our day in court. As Jim Walden told NBC News, 'With today's filings, the hunted becomes the hunter.'

Meanwhile, my initial three-month period of authorised stay

on my American visa was about to expire, so I had to file to renew it. In late 2016, I also filed a request for political asylum in the US. At my interview at Newark Asylum Office in Lyndhurst, New Jersey around one year later, asylum officers conducted extensive interviews: eight hours one day, six hours on a second day, and a third day that lasted another eight or so hours.

I figured that it was obvious that I would face harm if the US government returned me to Russia. The case of Sergei Magnitsky, a whistle-blower who died while awaiting trial in Russia, had alerted the world to the perils faced by opponents of the Putin regime. The danger to me was apparent, as I had similarly blown the whistle on Putin's wrongdoing in an extremely high-profile way.

Instead, one of the main impediments for asylum purposes was the baseless allegations by the Russian government that I was a criminal. A state-controlled Investigative Committee had accused me of numerous crimes, including the unauthorised sale of steroids, assisting athletes in using steroids, engaging in a criminal conspiracy and obstruction of the investigation. Commission of certain types of crimes can present a bar to obtaining asylum.

With the help of my lawyer Bo Cooper and his associates, I prepared as best I could for questions about my activities in Russia. I have an enthusiastic and excitable personality that isn't ideally suited to adversarial legal questioning. I tried to practise staying calm, explaining myself and listening and responding to the questions I was being asked.

Over the course of the interviews, the asylum officers peppered me with questions, reminding me at times of the FSKN investigators, whose accusations rolled over me like waves crashing on a beach. One officer probed whether I had committed crimes in Russia, a place she thought was on the other side of the moon, and also whether I may have committed crimes in the United States. After watching *Icarus* and browsing the internet, she had questions about whether, while working on the film, I had given Bryan Fogel my famous 'cocktail' containing poisonous steroids, or whether I committed wrongdoing by injecting him without a medical certificate.

How could I, with no medical qualifications whatsoever, concoct a 'cocktail' for athletes, using anabolic steroids, which were potent, lethal compounds? The officer showed me an internet article and told me to take a look: 'This bodybuilder died,' she said, 'and look what they found in his corpse: your favourite drugs, trenbolone and methenolone!'

This was a misunderstanding of the facts – and here is where the preparation kicked in. I tried my hardest to remain patient.

I replied that I was familiar with most of the scientific literature on the subject, and there was no evidence that a few milligrams of steroids per day were lethal. After all, the body naturally creates dozens of milligrams of steroids each day. A lot of 'doping', which sounds so insidious, is just bumping up levels of organic compounds found in every human metabolism. Obviously, tossing handfuls of pills down your throat and injecting yourself several times a day is dangerous, but so is drinking a litre of whisky and smoking two packs of cigarettes a day, and yet we haven't banned cigarettes and whisky.

The fact was that I hadn't induced anyone to use steroids; members of the national teams in some countries have been using them for years. My so-called cocktail was, in fact, a huge step forward, although I didn't dwell on this at length with the asylum officer. I had reduced steroid consumption tenfold, and we practically eliminated their side effects. I'm sure that in ten years, when people have stopped reading nonsense on the internet, pharmacies around the world will sell variants of my Sochi 'cocktail' instead of the modish and dangerous 'testosterone replacement therapy' that is sold all over the First World.

After the interviews were over, I was still nervous about the possible outcome. My life hung in the balance.

*

In March 2019, I was tending to my affairs and helping with ongoing investigations of doping violations, when my security team invited me to dinner at Delmonico's Steakhouse in New York. Everyone seemed joyful, and then they handed me my approval document – I had been granted political asylum, 'pursuant to section 208 of the Immigration and Nationality Act'.

My lawyers had scaled Mount Everest! Of course I was glad, but I wasn't euphoric. Three years ago, if I'd been holding this document in my hands, I would have jumped for joy, but now that I had the papers, I didn't know what to do with them. So much time had passed that it was as if they had delivered a year-old letter to an address where I no longer lived.

In just a few years, I've lived all over the United States, having been forced into hiding from the life I want to lead. I've been recognised only twice – once in a New York sports bar and once on a commuter train. Now, with the stroke of a pen, I have been granted asylum and can seek permanent residence, and even US citizenship in a few years.

It's hard to compare my life in America with my life in Russia. I sleep better in the US; I am not anxious and fearful as I was for my last few years in Moscow. I've slowed down a little, it's true, but that may be a function of aging. I can cook what I want, when I want. No one is bumping up against me in the kitchen. People ask me to compare how Americans go about their lives with how Russians live, but the difference is too vast – Russia and the USA are like completely different planets. There is a massive civilisation gap between the two countries, which I think is unlikely to be bridged, or even understood, in the foreseeable future. Can you compare a piranha to a sheepdog? I don't think so.

The worst thing about my life here is that my family, Veronika, Vasily and Marina, continue to live in Moscow, beyond my reach. I think about them every day and regret that we are, for the time being, forced to live separate lives. But this won't last forever – I am sure of it.

THE NEVER-ENDING WAR

On 22 October 2019, the US House of Representatives passed the Rodchenkov Anti-Doping Act of 2019 by unanimous consent. Citing the 'infamous Russian doping scandal during the 2014 Sochi Winter Olympics', House Judiciary Committee Chairman Jerry Nadler said the bill would establish 'appropriate criminal penalties and civil penalties for international doping fraud. In addition to imposing criminal penalties on the conspirators, the bill would authorise private civil actions for doping fraud, which would give athletes and corporate sponsors the right to sue in federal court to recover damages from individuals who may have defrauded competitions.'

That is the bark; the bite is fines of up to $1 million and ten-year jail terms.

To no one's surprise, the IOC and WADA hired Capitol Hill lobbyists to attempt to change the bill. WADA boss Sir Craig Reedie, who has since stepped down, complained that the proposed legislation tries to extend US criminal jurisdiction outside its borders. 'The area which is troublesome is the suggestion that American jurisdiction would go beyond the United States and might create liability in other parts of the world,' he said.

My lawyer, Jim Walden, argued that the IOC's position on the law proves they 'would rather host dirty games than have any-one else police doping fraud . . . If the IOC and WADA want to lobby US lawmakers on behalf of Russia's corrupt interests, that is a serious problem and I would encourage our congressmen and senators to be very wary of these efforts,' he said.

The bill represents a sea change in the war against doping. Instead of relying on WADA's civil enforcement of anti-doping rules, it brings law enforcement into the picture. Doping control currently targets only athletes, but coaches and team managers, or even a federation with a known history of abuse, often escape scrutiny. If they feel like answering questions they will, but if they don't, too bad. But if the American Senate follows the example of the House of Representatives and makes it US law, then actors known to have promoted doping fraud in competi-tion will be detained on arrival at the airport, or taken from the stadium to the police station.

At this point the authorities will tell them the nature of their crime, and how many years in prison they might face. At that moment, the sports boss or team manager would be stripped of his swagger and arrogance, and would start talking. In the hope of escaping with a suspended sentence, the accused conspirator will become a witness, and the war against doping will gain another foot soldier.

*

While the bill makes its way through US Congress, an equally serious battle, which could affect Russia's future in the Olympic Movement, has played out in front of WADA. In September 2018, WADA decided to reinstate RUSADA, without Russia having provided a copy of Moscow LIMS, the condition for reinstatement. LIMS contained suspect, atypical or positive findings for 2008 to 2011 and all analytical data for 2012 to 2015. This condition corresponded with previously enforced WADA guidelines stating that all positive and atypical results be uploaded to ADAMS in 2008, and that after 2012, all analyses be reported.

In 2017, WADA announced that it had obtained an authentic copy of the LIMS from a whistle-blower. The Russians refused to accept that version of the database, but refused to provide an 'authentic' version for comparison, insisting that the 'real' LIMS was crucial evidence in their ongoing criminal investigation of me.

Another condition for reinstating RUSADA required Russia to accept the McLaren Report and its conclusions. Reluctantly, without mentioning McLaren by name, Sports Minister Pavel Kolobkov informed WADA: 'The Russian Federation fully accepts the decision of the IOC Executive Board of 5 December 2017 that was made based on the findings of the Schmid Report.' Samuel Schmid, a member of the IOC's Ethics Commission, concluded that Russian authorities had engaged in a systematic doping programme for years, including at Sochi. He condemned 'the unprecedented nature of the cheating scheme and, as a consequence, exceptional damage to the integrity of the IOC, the Olympic Games and the entire Olympic Movement.'

It was after the Schmid Report that the IOC suspended the Russian Olympic Committee from the 2018 Winter Games in Pyeongchang and fined Russia $15 million. The Schmid Report resembled a watered-down version of the two 'independent person' reports from 2016 or, as I call it, 'McLaren for Dummies'. WADA accepted Kolobkov's statement as an admission of guilt for past crimes.

We now know that Russia was busily falsifying the LIMS database in preparation for handing it over to WADA at the end of 2018. When WADA's experts flew to Moscow to copy the LIMS, they were forbidden to do so; WADA returned in January 2019, which gave the Russians three more weeks to falsify results and even concoct and embed a phony text message exchange inside the LIMS, which purported to show that Dr Tim Sobolevsky and I had discussed extorting money from athletes, threatening to criminalise their urine samples.

Finally, on 9 December 2019, WADA's Intelligence and Investigations (I&I) Team disclosed the reckless LIMS tampering, and WADA's Compliance Committee recommended that Russia be banned from international major sporting events for the next four years, including the 2020 Summer Olympics in Tokyo and the 2022 Winter Games in Beijing.

'For too long, Russian doping has detracted from clean sport,' WADA president Reedie said in a statement. 'Russia was afforded every opportunity to get its house in order and re-join the global anti-doping community for the good of its athletes and of the integrity of sport, but it chose instead to continue in its stance of deception and denial.'

The details unearthed by WADA were damning. The data submitted by the Russians, they charged, were 'neither complete nor fully authentic . . . hundreds of presumptive adverse analytical findings that appear in the 2015 LIMS database have been removed from the 2019 LIMS database, and the related underlying raw data and PDF files have been deleted or altered.'

Most astonishingly, the Russians had deleted over 1,000 backup copies – the LIMS backed itself up at 4am every day, to protect the database from manipulation. On one hard disc, 93 per cent of the space was empty, with 450 LIMS copies and original files not just deleted but carefully 'zeroed' out, eliminating any possibility of the data being retrieved. This destroyed not just the analytical records on the LIMS, but all LIMS copies in Russia, and if this crucial data is lost who can say whether there are any clean athletes in Russia? Russia dug its own grave and has ruined the chances for any clean Russian athlete to compete.

President Vladimir Putin predictably slammed WADA's decision as a 'politically motivated' ruling that 'contradicted' the Olympic Charter. 'There is nothing to reproach the Russian Olympic Committee for and if there is no reproach towards this committee, the country should take part in competitions under its own flag,' he said. As usual, Russia will yet again fight its suspension in front of CAS.

It is an endless war.

The denouement of what Linda Helleland, a WADA

vice-president from Norway, called 'the biggest sports scandal the world has ever seen', is incredible: having been offered a path back to respectability in international sport, Russia opted not to take it. They were asked to hand over the raw data about their doping control between 2008 and 2016, and instead submitted a clumsily adulterated pack of lies, so artlessly counterfeited that it was almost as if they were begging to be caught.

We end where we began, in the world imagined by George Orwell. Russia loudly proclaims the doctrine of doublethink, being 'conscious of complete truthfulness while telling carefully constructed lies'. I am happy, finally, to be on the side of truth.

OPERATION SOCHI RESULTAT, STEP-BY-STEP

1. Participants

Dr Grigory Rodchenkov, director of the Sochi Olympic Laboratory.

Yuri Chizhov, second-in-command. Yuri's only job was night-time urine swapping.

Evgeny Kudryavtsev, head of reception, storage and the aliquotting (apportioning) section, on the first floor of the laboratory.

Evgeny Blokhin, FSB officer detailed to the Sochi laboratory. He disguised himself as a plumber during the day, going so far as to carry a case of tools.

Evgeny Antilsky, manager of the doping control station in the Olympic Village, where all urine samples ('the catch of the day') were consolidated for transportation to the laboratory.

Irina Rodionova, deputy director of the State Centre for the Sports Preparation of the National Teams of Russia (CSP). She collected and stored clean urine samples to be swapped in

Sochi, coordinated the swapping scheme and texted scans of athletes' doping control forms to the Olympic laboratory after their urine tests.

2. Prior to the Olympics

- In the summer of 2013, we collected clean urine samples from as many as 75 winter sports athletes, even before it was known who would be on the Olympic team. The athletes deposited their samples in watertight containers, which is how we ended up with soda bottles in the freezers in our FSB Command Centre in Sochi.
- The athletes froze their urine before sending it to Irina Rodionova in Moscow.
- Rodionova (or an aide) delivered the urine to me at the Moscow Anti-Doping Centre.
- Laboratory experts double-checked that the samples were negative – in other words 'clean'.
- If the samples were clean, Irina stored them at an unknown secure location at the CSP – the 'clean urine bank', as Richard McLaren later called it.
- Rodionova forwarded the samples to the FSB Sochi Command Centre in late January 2014.
- It seems that as many as 500 urine samples arrived at the Sochi Command Centre. On 1 February 2014, Evgeny Blokhin and I visited the centre and conducted a complete inspection of the freezers and their contents.

3. Testing Day at the Olympic Games

3.1 Step One – At the Doping Control Station

- An athlete selected for testing arrives at the doping control station, accompanied by the team physician.
- There is a manned security entrance at the station, where the athlete must produce their Olympic accreditation and the testing notification document.
- Security checks in the athlete, along with an accompanying person. They are escorted to a waiting area with chairs, a television and drinks.
- When the athlete is ready, they notify the Doping Control Manager and are directed to a specific table where they are instructed on sampling procedures. A doping control officer (DCO) fills out the doping control form (DCF).
- The athlete then selects a carton of BEREG-kit bottles, an A and a B bottle and a sealed plastic cup for urine collection.
- The athlete unwraps the urine collection cup and inspects it, before depositing a urine sample in the collection cup while being observed by the DCO. The officer enters the total volume of urine collected into the DCF.
- The athlete returns to the collection area, opens the cardboard box and inspects the A and B BEREG-kit bottles. They unwrap the bottles, remove a red security ring and distribute the urine from the collection cup into the A and B bottles.
- The athlete must deposit around 30ml into the B bottle, which is marked with a line on a blue label.

- The athlete must then deposit around 60ml into the A sample, marked with a line on a red label.
- If there is enough urine left in the collection cup, it is divided between the A and B bottles, until around 5–10ml remains to test for specific gravity, which measures the urine's relative density to water.
- The athlete then seals the A and B bottles with numbered caps from the carton and passes them to the doping control officer for a leak check.
- The DCO measures the specific gravity of the leftover urine, poured from the collection cap, and enters the readings in the DCF.
- It is important to note that the DCF specifies the total volume of urine deposited into the collection cup, but not the exact volume poured into the A and B bottles. The sum of the A and B volumes does not match the total amount of urine voided by the athlete, since a portion was left in the collection cup for the specific gravity measurement and then disposed of.
- The athlete departs with their copy of the DCF, which lists the athlete's name, personal data, code number, specific gravity and total volume.
- The athlete or accompanying person takes a photo of the doping control form.
- An FSB staffer at the doping station takes a second photo of the DCF, as a precautionary measure.

3.2 Step Two – After the Doping Control Station

- Photos of the doping control forms are sent to Irina Rodionova.
- Irina texts the DCF scans to Dr Rodchenkov and his secretaries, and then calls to confirm which athletes have given samples.
- An anonymous FSB coordinator sends DCF to Evgeny Blokhin and Yuri Chizhov.

3.3 Step Three – At the Laboratory and FSB Command Centre

- Grigory, Yuri, Evgeny Kudryavtsev and Evgeny Blokhin note the number of samples to be swapped each night, their code numbers, the athletes' names and which sports are represented.
- Grigory and Yuri confer with Blokhin to determine which athletes' 'clean' samples need to be delivered to the Olympic laboratory. Grigory prepares a 'Table of the Day', with athletes' names, code numbers, specific gravities and volumes needed to fill the A and B bottles.
- At around 5pm, Blokhin retrieves plastic bags with the athletes' 'clean' urine from the freezer in the Command Centre and brings them to Room 124 of the laboratory, where they are thawed. This can take an hour, or less if we immerse the plastic soda bottles in warm water.
- Once thawed, the specimens are poured into 250-ml glass beakers (marked as 1, 2, 3, etc, according to the 'Table of the Day'). Chizhov measures the samples' specific gravities using the same Asahi densitometer as the doping control station.

- If the specific gravity of the negative urine is lower than the reading in the DCF, we add sodium chloride; if it is higher, we add distilled water. If the specific gravity matches or is within 0.002 points of the original sample, everything is fine.

3.4 Step Four – Consolidation of the Samples in the Olympic Village and Delivery to the Laboratory

- When the doping control station has finished its collection session, chain of custody (CoC) forms are filled out and the urine samples are packed in bags. These are sealed and delivered to a temporary storage area at the main doping control station inside the Olympic Village polyclinic.
- During the day, samples accumulate at the polyclinic. At around midnight, Evgeny Antilsky calls the laboratory and informs us that we should expect the arrival of the minivan full of samples in the next 15 minutes.
- Grigory and Yuri make sure that the laboratory is clear of foreign observers. Only Thierry Boghosian, the WADA independent observer, is allowed to enter the reception and sample storage zones, where each opening of a door or of a freezer is logged and recorded by numerous cameras.

3.5. Step Five – The Night Swap

- The samples arrive at around 1am. The minivan enters the laboratory perimeter and stops at a special door reserved for DCOs. At the laboratory reception, the samples and documentation are checked and labelled. The volumes of the A and B bottles are measured and the chain of custody is documented.

All data is automatically downloaded to LIMS (the Laboratory Information Management System).

- Grigory, Yuri and Evgeny move into Room 124.
- At reception, the A and B bottles are loaded onto different carts. Evgeny Kudryavtsev wheels the B bottles to a locked storage room containing freezers in the designated long-term storage zone.
- Kudryavtsev takes the selected B bottles off the cart and slips them into his lab coat, leaving the other B bottles in the long-term storage zone.
- Returning to reception, Kudryavtsev wheels the A sample cart to Room 125, the aliquotting room, where the caps are opened.
- There is a circular drilled hole (the 'mousehole') in the wall between Room 124 and Room 125, large enough to pass BEREG-kit bottles through. To avoid detection, it is covered by a circular plastic cap, giving it the appearance of an inoperative power outlet, and hidden behind a filing cabinet.
- Kudryavtsev selects matched A and B bottles, and feeds those through the hole, from Room 125 to Room 124.
- Chizhov receives the A and B bottles in the operations room, Room 124.
- Rodchenkov double-checks that the A and B bottles have the correct matching code numbers, ensures they look acceptable and records the volumes in his 'Table of the Day'.
- Grigory hands the B bottles to Evgeny Blokhin, who returns to the FSB Command Centre where the caps are removed.
- Yuri had earlier prepared the required volumes of urine to be swapped out in numbered 250-ml glass beakers. He again

checks the specific gravity of the thawed urine, before empty-ing the A bottle and rinsing it.

- Because there is no running water or drain in the operations room, we haul five-litre bottles of distilled water from an upper floor to use during swapping. The used water is poured into plastic tubs and the dirty water into toilets along the corridor.

- Grigory, Evgeny K. and Yuri smoke a cigarette and drink coffee while they wait for Evgeny Blokhin to return with opened B bottles, that now have an unattached cap on top of each bottle.

- Since the ring of metal teeth inside the plastic cap were scratched during opening, new metal parts are inserted inside the plastic cap of each B bottle. We had earlier collected several hundred of those rings from the crushed caps of A bottles.

- Grigory thoroughly sanitises the inside of the B bottle plastic cap, while Yuri washes the B bottles.

- Paired and cleaned A and B bottles with caps are lined up in front of Grigory on his table, and then all numbers, names, volumes and specific gravities are checked against the 'Table of the Day'.

- Grigory and Yuri check the specific gravity of each urine speci-men again.

- Grigory then pours clean (negative and unthawed) urine into the A and B bottles, making sure the volume matches that listed in the 'Table of the Day'. Yuri observes Grigory closely; it is 4 or 5am and everyone is tired and mistake-prone.

- A bottle stopper is returned to the A bottle, and the B bottle receives a seemingly intact plastic cap. Grigory tightens it and checks for leaks.

- Yuri passes the A and B bottles back through the mousehole to the controlled zone, where Evgeny Kudryavtsev receives them in Room 125.
- Kudryavtsev deposits the A bottles in the aliquoting room and takes the B bottles to the designated long-term storage zone.
- Dr Rodchenkov destroys the 'Table of the Day', tearing it into small pieces and distributing them among the laboratory trash cans. He also deletes scans of DCFs from his telephone, as do Yuri and the laboratory secretary.
- Grigory telephones Irina Rodionova to report that the session has gone according to plan.

ABBREVIATIONS

AAF – Adverse analytical finding: a 'positive' analytical result reported to ADAMS. The testing authorities investigate each AAF to determine if an ADRV has occurred.

ABP – Athlete biological passport. This practice documents suspicious deviations of an athlete's blood and urine parameters, in relation to his or her steroidal profile. No single data point constitutes a positive result, but ADRV can be based on a statistical evaluation of several (minimum 5 to 7) data points.

ADAMS – Anti-Doping Administration and Management System. An international database intended to monitor athletes' whereabouts and competition plans, ADAMS helps generate plans for international testing authorities. Laboratories download their analytical results to ADAMS.

ADC – Anti-Doping Centre, Moscow; my WADA-accredited laboratory, part of the Russian Ministry of Sport.

ADRV – Anti-doping rule violation, which triggers hearings and sanctions, based on an AAF.

ARAF – All-Russian Athletics Federation, the governing body for Russian track and field. Suspended from international competition by the IAAF in November 2015 and not yet reinstated.

ARD – German TV network that aired a shocking documentary on 3 December 2014 about widespread doping by Russian athletes.

CAS – Court of Arbitration for Sport, Lausanne. CAS resolves disputes among athletes, teams, national and international sports organisations – for example, between the International Olympic Committee and WADA.

CoC – Chain of custody form, a document initiated at a doping control station, to demonstrate the uninterrupted control of urine and blood samples from collection to transportation and reception in the laboratory. Athletes and coaches do not see the CoC form.

CSP – Centre for the Sports Preparation of the National Teams of Russia. Supported by the Ministry of Sport and employing thousands of athletes and coaches, the CSP pays salaries, bonuses and incentives and covers all athletes' costs associated with travelling, training camps, participation in competition and the purchase of equipment.

DCO – Doping control officer, the person authorised to collect doping control samples.

DCF – Doping control form, the most important document completed inside the doping control station. The athlete receives a copy, and the local doping control laboratory receives a blind copy, without the athlete's name, identifying data or signature.

DCS – Doping control station, a special facility where the DCOs collect urine and blood samples.

EPO – Erythropoietin or ESA (erythropoietin-stimulating agents) are effective peptides that increase haemoglobin concentration in the bloodstream.

FIS – International Ski Federation, for cross-country and alpine events.

FSB – Federal Security Service, the successor to the KGB after the dissolution of the USSR.

FSKN – Federal Drug Control Service, the corrupt Russian anti-narcotics police, disbanded in 2016.

GC-MS – Gas chromatography–mass spectrometry, sophisticated analytical instrumentation for detecting doping substances.

HGH – Human growth hormone; strengthens joints and tendons, burns fat and improves muscle structure. HGH is widely believed to prevent injury and speed recovery from injury.

IAAF – International Association of Athletics Federations, Monte Carlo. The international governing body for track and field, now renamed WA (World Athletics).

IBU – International Biathlon Union, Salzburg, Austria.

IDTM – International Drug and Testing Management, the Swedish sample collection authority working in Russia.

IO – Independent observer, assigned by WADA to major multisport events (for example, the Olympics, World Championships or Commonwealth Games).

IOC – International Olympic Committee, Lausanne.

IRTP – International Registered Testing Pool, elite athletes who are tested on a regular basis, based in part on risk assessment for doping.

ISL – International Standard for Laboratories, published by WADA.

ITP – Initial testing procedures are used in WADA-accredited laboratories to analyse samples, covering doping substances of different classes and origin. Each ITP requires a separate aliquot (portion of urine). Usually, a laboratory uses five to seven aliquots for various types of analysis.

IWF – International Weightlifting Federation, Budapest, Hungary.

KGB – Committee for State Security in the USSR, converted to FSB after the dissolution of the USSR.

LDP – The Laboratory Documentation Package contains detailed information on the analysis performed in a WADA-accredited laboratory. As a rule, LDP is based on the LIMS data and provided to an athlete or testing authority on request, revealing authentic documentation to prove AAF.

LIMS – Laboratory Information Management System; a complete, digitised record of sample reception, analysis and results, shared with ADAMS. Implemented at the Moscow ADC in 2009. Printouts and forms from LIMS are the basis of LDP.

MSU – Moscow State University. My alma mater. I graduated from the chemistry department in 1982. MGU is where I met my wife Veronika, who was pursuing a degree in physics.

NADO – National Anti-Doping Organisation, the independent testing authorities in each country, like USADA in USA, RUSADA in Russian and UKAD – UK Anti-Doping – in Great Britain.

NOC – National Olympic Committee, recognised by the IOC.

PB – Personal best, a personal record in swimming, skating or track and field.

PED – Performance-enhancing drug, a term I try to avoid using because it blurs definitions. For instance, WADA prohibits the use of diuretics, which are not PEDs, while caffeine, a known PED, does not appear on WADA's Prohibited List of doping substances.

PWC – Medizinische Testverfahren im Sport. International sample collection authority for winter sports, based in Munich, Germany. PWC performs the same functions as IDTM does in summer sports.

RUSADA – Russian Anti-Doping Agency, established in 2008. The first RUSADA officials were trained at USADA, in Colorado Springs.

TDP – Test distribution plan, based on intelligence and risk assessment. In theory, testing authorities prepare TDPs to assure the efficacy of doping control measures.

T/E – Testosterone to epi-Testosterone ratio, established in 1983 by Professor Manfred Donike as a main parameter in urinary steroid profile, indicating the possible abuse of testosterone. The steroid profile became part of the athlete biological passport in 2014.

TUE – Therapeutic use exemption allows athletes to take medicines – for example, cold remedies with ephedrines – for health reasons. A TUE often triggers reporting AAF, but does not constitute an ADRV.

UCI – Union Cycliste Internationale, the governing body in cycling.

USADA – The United States Anti-Doping Agency, based in Colorado Springs, Colorado.

VNIIFK – The All-Union (now All-Russian) Scientific and Research Institute for Physical Culture in Moscow, part of the Ministry of Sport. Home to Russia's first anti-doping laboratory, established in 1971 and accredited by the IOC in 1980 before the Olympic Games in Moscow.

WADA – The World Anti-Doping Agency, established November 1999.

INDEX

Page references in *italics* indicate images.
GR indicates Grigory Rodchenkov.